Modern Java

Java 7 and Polyglot Programming on the JVM

Adam L. Davis

Modern Java

Java 7 and Polyglot Programming on the JVM

Adam L. Davis

This book is for sale at http://leanpub.com/modernjava

This version was published on 2014-01-31

ISBN 978-1494973988

Tweet This Book!

Please help Adam L. Davis by spreading the word about this book on Twitter!

The suggested hashtag for this book is #modernjava.

Find out what other people are saying about the book by clicking on this link to search for this hashtag on Twitter:

https://twitter.com/search?q=#modernjava

Also By Adam L. Davis

What's New in Java 8

Modern Programming Made Easy

Dedicated to my wife and son.

Contents

Introduction i
    Always be learning i
    Who is this book for? i
    What is this book about? i
    What this book is not about i

Tech Predictions iii
    Multi-core Processors are Commonplace iii
    Multi-touch Becomes Standard iii
    Linux has Arrived iii
    Smart Phones will be Old Hat iii

Part I: Java 1

Java 3
    History 3
    Open-ness 3
    The Java Ecosystem 4

Java 5 & 6 5
    Java 1.5 5
    Java 1.6 7

Java 7 9
    Language Updates 9
    Fork/Join 12
    New IO (nio) 14
    JVM Benefits 15
    Performance Benefits 15
    Backwards Compatibility 16

Java's Future 17
    Overview 17
    New Date and Time API 17

Lambda Expressions 17
Method References 18
Default Methods 19
Map/Reduce 19
Parallel Array 20
Introducing Dollar 22

Guava **25**
Collections 25
Objects 25
Concurrency 26
Functional Programming 26
Optional 27
Other Useful Classes 27

Maven **29**
What is Maven? 29
Using Maven 29
Starting a New Project 29
Lifecycle 30
Executing Code 31
Deploying to Maven Central 32

Continuous Development and Testing **33**
Definitions 33
Types of Testing 34
Test Frameworks 34
Arquillian 35
Automated Build Systems 35

JUnit **37**
What is JUnit? 37
Hamcrest 37
Assumptions 38
The Beauty of JUnit Theories 38

Concurrency in Java **41**
State of Concurrent Programming in Java 41
Prominent Models for Concurrency 41
Synchronize in Java 41
Java Futures 42
STM in Clojure 42
Actors 43
Groovy GPars 43

Part II: JVM Languages 45

Other JVM Languages 47
Why use non-Java Languages? 47
Polyglot Programming 48
Dynamic Languages, Refactoring IDE, pick one... 48
Edge-Craft 49
Java.next(): Groovy vs. Scala 49

Groovy 53
What is Groovy? 53
Compact Syntax 53
List and Map Definitions 53
Easy Properties 54
GString 54
Closures 55
A Better Switch 55
Gotcha's 56
Groovy 1.8 57
Groovy 2.0 57
Static Type Checking 57

Design Patterns in Groovy 59
Strategy Pattern 59
Iterators 60
DSL's 61
Meta-programming 62
Command pattern 62
Delegation 63

The Groovy Ecosystem 65
Web and UI Frameworks 65
Cloud Computing Frameworks 65
Build Frameworks 65
Testing Frameworks/Code Analysis 66
Concurrency 66
Honorable Mentions 66

Gradle 67
Projects and Tasks 67
Plugins 68
Maven Dependencies 68

Spock 71

Introduction 71
A Simple Test 71
Mocking 72
Lists or Tables of Data 72
Expecting Exceptions 73
Conclusion 74

Scala **75**
What is Scala? 75
Hello World 75
Everything's an object 76
Everything's an expression 76
Match is Switch on Steroids 77
Traits as Mixins 78
List and Apply 79
Tuples 80
Maps 81
For Expressions 82
Scala 2.9 84
Scala 2.10 85

Design Patterns in Scala **87**
Strategy Pattern 87
Iterators 88
DSL's 89
Metaprogramming in Scala 90

The Scala Ecosystem **93**
Web Frameworks 93
ORM Frameworks 93
Build frameworks 94
Testing frameworks/Code Analysis 94
Concurrency 94
Honorable Mentions 95

Part III: The Web **97**

JVM Clouds **99**
Cloudbees 99
CloudFoundry 99
Heroku 100
Jelastic 100
Commonalities 100

Grails **101**
    What is Grails? 101
    Quick Overview of Grails 101
    Plugins 103
    What's New in Grails 2.0? 103
    Cloud 105
    Groovy Mailgun in Heroku 105

Play Framework 2 . . . . **109**
    What is Play? 109
    Quick Overview of Play 109
    Controllers, Views, Forms 110
    ORM 110
    Play 1.x 110
    Play 2.0 111
    Typesafe Activator 111

RESTful web-services **113**
    REST in Groovy 113
    REST in Scala 114
    JAX-RS 1.0 115
    JAX-RS 2.0 115

Final Thoughts **119**
    The State of the JVM 119
    The Future 119
    Contact the Author 119

Appendix: Groovy for Java Devs **121**

Appendix: Scala for Java Devs **123**

Introduction

Always be learning

It's an exciting time to be a programmer, especially in the JVM space. Java 7 is widely used and Java 8 is closer to completion while other JVM languages, like Groovy and Scala, have been increasing in popularity. With the accelerating pace of change in technology, it is important as a programmer to always be learning and looking forward to the latest and greatest technology.

Who is this book for?

This book is meant for Java programmers or aspiring programmers who want to know about the latest Java and JVM technology.

What is this book about?

This book should help you understand the latest in Java 7; concurrent programming; build, testing, and web frameworks; and the best JVM languages so you can advance your career in software development.

What this book is not about

This book will not cover the basics of HTML, CSS, SQL, or any other non-JVM languages and will assume you know the basics of programming.

Tech Predictions

It's important to think ahead in this ever changing world, especially as a programmer. Making predictions of technology in the near future is somewhat easy, but it gets more difficult when you predict five years ahead or more. Here are some predictions relevant to programmers (which are basically just observations of current trends circa 2014):

Multi-core Processors are Commonplace

Dual-cores are already showing up in our smart-phones, and due to the simple progression of an updated "Moore's law", we should have 16-cores in smart-phones and tablets by 2020. This will make concurrent programming more mainstream as many of us already know. So learning about modern concurrent programming approaches (agents, immutability, etc.) is important.

Multi-touch Becomes Standard

It seems almost self-evident that multi-touch will become the standard interaction model. Tablets and smart-phones are soaring in popularity, and multi-touch is even moving into the dwindling desktop and laptop markets. It makes sense then to stop assuming mouse and/or keyboard interaction if you deal with any sort of user-interface design. Java on Android is an obvious winner, but so are HTML5-based solutions like Sencha Touch[1].

Linux has Arrived

With Ubuntu, Android, and ChromeOS, Linux is already forging ahead into mainstream technology. Does this effect you? Probably not if you're a web-developer, but if you develop apps for Windows or OSX, you will need to diversify. Linux (in its many different forms) might just (finally) disrupt the OS market.

Smart Phones will be Old Hat

To some people smart-phones are already old news; the big new thing is Google Glass[2] or smart watches like Pebble[3]. There will probably be several competitors to Google Glass and Pebble, so the "glasses" and/or smart-watch market might look much like the smart-phone market of today.

---

[1]http://www.sencha.com/products/touch
[2]http://en.wikipedia.org/wiki/Project_Glass
[3]https://getpebble.com/

Part I: Java

Java

History

Java™ was first developed in the 90's by James Gosling. It borrows much of its syntax from C and C++ to be more appealing to existing programmers at the time. Java was owned by Sun Microsystems which was then acquired by Oracle in 2010.

Java is a *statically typed, object-oriented* language. Statically typed means every variable and parameter must have a defined type (as opposed to languages like Javascript which are dynamically typed). Object-oriented (OO), means that data and functions are grouped together into objects (functions are usually referred to as *methods* in OO languages).

Java code is compiled to byte-code which runs on a virtual machine (the Java Virtual Machine, JVM). The virtual machine handles garbage collection and allows Java to be compiled once, and run on any OS or hardware that has a JVM. This is an advantage over C/C++ which has to be compiled directly to machine code and has no automatic garbage collection (the programmer needs to allocate and deallocate memory).

The standard implementation of Java comes in two different packages, the JRE (Java Runtime Environment) and the JDK (Java Developement Kit). The JRE is strictly for running Java as an end user, while the JDK is for developing Java code. The JDK comes with the "javac" command for compiling Java code to byte-code, among other things.

At the time of writing, Java is one of the most popular programming languages in use[4], particularly for server-side web applications.

Open-ness

In an attempt to make Java more open and community based, Sun Microsystems started the Java Community Process (JCP), which allows a somewhat democratic evolution of Java and JVM specifications. Also, Sun relicensed most of its Java technologies under the GNU General Public License in May 2007 which has resulted in multiple open-source implementations of the JVM (OpenJDK is the official one). Although Sun has many patents on some aspects of the JVM, historically it has not used these patents to sue other companies, which has allowed a healthy ecosystem of competing JVM's to emerge. Although Oracle sued Google over its use of Java in Android, Oracle eventually lost the case in May 2012[5].

---

[4]http://www.tiobe.com/index.php/content/paperinfo/tpci/index.html

[5]http://news.cnet.com/8301-1023_3-57440235-93/

Generally when we refer to the JVM, we are referring Oracle's JVM, but OpenJDK or any other JVM can be used.

The Java Ecosystem

The Java Ecosystem is huge. It is mainly composed of JVM's, libraries, tools, and IDE's. It is so huge, there's no way to really summarize it in one book, but we will cover some of the highlights.

The three most popular IDE's are (in no particular order):

- Eclipse[6] - Open-source project by the Eclipse Foundation.
- NetBeans[7] - Sun's (now Oracle's) open-source Java IDE.
- IntelliJ IDEA[8] - A commercial IDE with a community edition.

We will discuss some of the more promising new libraries and tools in the Java ecosystem, such as the following:

- Maven, gradle and other build tools.
- Libraries for concurrent programming.
- JUnit, spock and other test frameworks.
- Groovy, Scala, and other JVM languages.
- Grails, Play, and other web-frameworks.
- JVM Cloud providers.

---

[6]http://eclipse.org/
[7]http://netbeans.org/
[8]https://www.jetbrains.com/idea/

Java 5 & 6

Java 1.5

Java 5 added several new features to the language. If you're not familiar with Java 5 or would like a refresher, keep reading. We're going to assume you understand these concepts in the remainder of the book.

Java 5 added the following features:

- Generics
- Annotations
- More concise `for` loops
- Static imports
- Autoboxing/unboxing
- Enumerations
- Varargs
- Concurrency utilities in package `java.util.concurrent`

Generics

Generics were a huge addition to the language. They improved the type-safety of Java, but also added a lot of complexity to the language.

Generics are used most commonly to specify what type a Collection holds. This reduces the need for casting and improves type-safety. For example, declaring a `List` of Strings is the following:

```
1  List<String> strings = new ArrayList<String>();
```

Declaring a Map of `Long` to `String` would appear as the following:

```
1  Map<Long,String> map = new HashMap<Long,String>();
```

The need to repeat the generic type twice in the declaration is one of Java's harshest criticisms. However various libraries, such as Google's guava, make this less painful by using static methods. For example declaring the above map would be as simple as the following:

```
1   Map<Long,String> map = Maps.newHashMap();
```

Also, Java 7 will ameliorate this situation with the *diamond operator*, which we will discuss later.

Annotations

Java annotations allow you to add meta-information to Java code that can be used by the compiler, various API's, or even your own code at runtime.

The most common annotation you will see is the `@Override` annotation which declares to the compiler that you are overriding a method. This is useful because it will cause a compile-time error if you mistype the method name for example.

Other useful annotations are those in `javax.annotation` such as `@Nonnull` and `@Nonnegative` which declare your intentions.

Annotations such as `@Autowired` and `@Inject` are used by direct-injection frameworks like Spring and Google Guice[9], respectively, to reduce "wiring" code.

More concise for loops

You can write for loops in a concise way for an array or any class that implements `Iterable`. For example:

```
1   String[] strArray = {"a", "b", "c"};
2   for (String str : strArray)
3           out.println(str);
```

"Wait, don't you need a System there?" you're probably thinking. Not necessarily in Java 5 with the *static import* feature.

Static import

In Java 5 you can use the words `import static` to import a static member of another class. This can help your code be more concise as shown in the above section. To do this, you would need the following at the top of the class file:

```
1   import static java.lang.System.out;
```

However, the creators of Java recommend you use static import very sparingly[10], so don't get carried away.

---

[9]http://code.google.com/p/google-guice/

[10]http://docs.oracle.com/javase/1.5.0/docs/guide/language/static-import.html

Autoboxing, Enums, Varargs

Autoboxing

The Java compiler will automatically wrap a primitive type in the corresponding object when it's necessary. For example, when assigning a variable or passing in parameters to a function, as in the following: `printSpaced(1, 2, 3)`

Unboxing

This is simply the reverse of Autoboxing. The Java compiler will unwrap an object to the corresponding primitive type when possible. For example, the following code would work:
`double d = new Double(1.1) + new Double(2.2)`

Enums

The enum keyword creates a typesafe, ordered list of values. For example, `enum Letter { A, B, C; }`

Varargs

You can declare a method's last parameter with an elipse (. . .) and it will be interpreted to accept any number of parameters (including zero) and convert them into an array in your method. For example, see the following code:

void printSpaced(Object... objects) { for (Object o : objects) out.print(o + " "); }

Putting it all together, you have the following code (with output in comments):

```
printSpaced(Letter.A, Letter.B, Letter.C); // A B C
printSpaced(1, 2, 3); // 1 2 3
```

Concurrency utilities

These will be discussed in later chapters (`ExecutorService` and `Future`).

Java 1.6

Java 6 did not have as many big changes as Java 5, but it did add the following:

- **Web Services** - First-class support for writing XML web services.
- **Scripting** - the ability to plug-in scripting engines (for Javascript, Ruby, and Groovy for example).
- **Java DB** (Apache Derby) is co-bundled in the JRE.
- **JDBC 4.0** adds many feature additions like special support for XML as an SQL datatype and better integration of Binary Large OBjects (BLOBs) and Character Large OBjects (CLOBs).

- **More Desktop APIs** - SwingWorker, JTable, and more.
- **Monitoring and Management** - Jhat for forensic explorations of core dumps.
- **Compiler Access** - The compiler API opens up programmatic access to javac for in-process compilation of dynamically generated Java code.
- **Override interface methods** - The @Override annotation can be used to declare you're overriding an interface method.

Java 7

As Oracle will no longer provide free updates to Java 6 (as of Feb. 2013), Java 7 is now the de-facto standard version of Java. It is already in use in many production systems, so if you are currently using Java 6, it's time to upgrade. Java 7 has some performance benefits and new features[11] that many programmers have been expecting for years.

Language Updates

The following features have been added to Java the language:

- Diamond Operator
- Strings in switch
- Automatic resource management
- Improved Exception handling
- Numbers with underscores

Diamond Operator

The *Diamond Operator* simplifies the declaration of generic classes. The generic types are inferred from the definition of the field or variable. For example, in the following code, the second line is now equivalent to the first in Java 7:

```
1  Map<String, List<Double>> nums = new HashMap<String, List<Double>> ();
2  Map<String, List<Double>> nums = new HashMap <> ();
```

Strings in Switch

You can now use *Strings in switch* statements. For example, the following code would compile and work in Java 7:

---

[11]http://openjdk.java.net/projects/jdk7/features/

```
1   public static <T> Collection<T> makeNew(String type, Class<T> tClass) {
2           switch (type) {
3           case "set":
4                   return new HashSet<>();
5           case "lset":
6                   return new LinkedHashSet<>();
7           case "treeset":
8                   return new TreeSet<>();
9           case "vector":
10                  return new Vector<>();
11          case "array":
12                  return new ArrayList<>();
13          case "deque":
14          case "queue":
15          case "list":
16          default:
17                  return new LinkedList<>();
18          }
19  }
```

As seen above, Strings can now be used just like any primitive would in a switch statement.

 Github Repo

You can find the source-code for these examples on github modern-java-examples[12].

Automatic resource management

The new *Automatic resource management* feature makes dealing with resources, such as files, much easier. Before Java 7 you needed to explicitly close all open streams, causing some very verbose code. Now you can just do the following:

---

[12]https://github.com/adamd/modern-java-examples

```
1   public void writeWithTry() {
2           try (FileOutputStream fos = new FileOutputStream("books.txt");
3                        DataOutputStream dos = new DataOutputStream(fos)) {
4               dos.writeUTF("Modern Java");
5           } catch (IOException e) {
6               // log the exception
7           }
8   }
```

Improved Exception handling

Improved Exception handling in Java 7 means that you can catch more than one exception in one catch statement. Previously, you had to write a different catch block for each exception. This may seem trivial, but will make Java development somewhat easier. Here's an example of the new style:

```
1   public static Integer fetchURLAsInteger(String urlString) {
2           try {
3
4                   URL url = new URL(urlString);
5                   String str = url.openConnection().getContent().toString();
6                   return Integer.parseInt(str);
7
8           } catch (NullPointerException | NumberFormatException | IOException e) {
9                   return null;
10          }
11  }
```

The above code would fetch content from the given url and attempt to convert it to an Integer. If anything goes wrong it returns null. Although this is a contrived example, similar situations do occur in real code.

Numbers with underscores

Numbers with underscores is exactly what you think. Humans have a hard time reading long streams of numbers, so Java 7 allows you to put underscores in numeric literals to make them easier to understand. For example, three million would be written as follows:

```
1   int lemmings = 3_000_000;
```

Fork/Join

There are new Java concurrency APIs (JSR 166y) referred to as the **Fork-join framework**. It is designed for tasks that can be broken down and takes advantage of multiple processors. The core classes are the following (all located in `java.util.concurrent`):

- `ForkJoinPool`: An ExecutorService for running ForkJoinTasks and managing and monitoring the tasks.
- `ForkJoinTask`: This represents the abstract task that runs within the ForkJoinPool.
- `RecursiveTask`: This is a subclass of ForkJoinTask whose compute method returns some value.
- `RecursiveAction`: This is a subclass of ForkJoinTask whose compute method does not return any value.

As an example of using this framework, let's find the sum of 2000 integers. This is a trivial example but will hopefully demonstrate proper use of the ForkJoin framework.

In this example we will divide the array of integers in half and assign each half to a `RecursiveTask`. If the array size is less than 20 elements then we assign it to another RecursiveTask that computes the sum of the array.

Here is the RecursiveTask for computing the sum:

```java
class SumCalculatorTask extends RecursiveTask<Integer>{
    int [] numbers;
    SumCalculatorTask(int[] numbers){
        this.numbers = numbers;
    }


    @Override
    protected Integer compute() {
        int sum = 0;
        for (int i : numbers){
            sum += i;
        }
        return sum;
    }
}
```

The compute method has to be overridden with the actual task to be performed. In the above case its iterate through the elements of the array and return the computed sum.

We create a RecursiveTask for dividing the array into two parts and assign each part to another RecursiveTask for further dividing. We continue dividing the array and stop dividing when the array has less than 20 elements.

```
1    class NumberDividerTask extends RecursiveTask<Integer>{
2           int [] numbers;
3           NumberDividerTask(int [] numbers){
4                  this.numbers = numbers;
5           }
6
7           @Override
8           protected Integer compute() {
9                  int sum = 0;
10                 List<RecursiveTask<Integer>> forks = new ArrayList<>();
11                 if (numbers.length > 20){
12                        NumberDividerTask task1 =
13                               new NumberDividerTask(Arrays
14                                 .copyOfRange(numbers, 0, numbers.length/2));
15                        NumberDividerTask task2 =
16                               new NumberDividerTask(Arrays
17                                 .copyOfRange(numbers, numbers.length/2, numbers.length));
18                        forks.add(task1);
19                        forks.add(task2);
20                        task1.fork();
21                        task2.fork();
22                 } else {
23                        SumCalculatorTask sumCalcTask = new SumCalculatorTask(numbers);
24                        forks.add(sumCalcTask);
25                        sumCalcTask.fork();
26                 }
27                 //Combine the result from all the tasks
28                 for (RecursiveTask<Integer> task : forks) {
29                        sum += task.join();
30                 }
31                 return sum;
32          }
33   }
```

The above NumberDividerTask spawns either two other NumberDividerTask's or a SumCalculatorTask. Each task keeps a track of the sub-tasks it has created. At the end of the task we wait for all the tasks in the forks list to finish by invoking the join() method and compute the sum of those values returned from the sub-tasks.

To invoke the above defined tasks we make use of ForkJoinPool and create a NumberDividerTask task by giving it the array whose sum we wish to compute.

```
1  public class ForkJoinTest {
2          static ForkJoinPool forkJoinPool = new ForkJoinPool();
3          public static final int LENGTH = 2000;
4
5          public static void main(String[] args) {
6                  int [] numbers = new int[LENGTH];
7                  // Create  an array with some values.
8                  for(int i=0; i<LENGTH; i++){
9                          numbers[i] = i * 2;
10                 }
11                 int sum = forkJoinPool.invoke(new NumberDividerTask(numbers));
12
13                 System.out.println("Sum: "+sum);
14         }
15 }
```

After running the above code the output should be: Sum: 3998000.

Although this is a simple example, the same concept could be applied to any "divide and conquer" algorithm.

New IO (nio)

Java 7 adds several new classes and interfaces for manipulating files and file-systems. This new API allows developers to access many low-level OS operations that were not available from the Java API before, such as the WatchService and the ability to create links (in *nix operating systems).

The following list defines some of the most important classes and interfaces of the NIO API:

Files This class consists exclusively of static methods that operate on files, directories, or other types of files.

FileStore
    Storage for files.

FileSystem
    Provides an interface to a file system and is the factory for objects to access files and other objects in the file system.

FileSystems
    Factory methods for file systems.

LinkPermission
    The Permission class for link creation operations.

Paths

This class consists exclusively of static methods that return a Path by converting a path string or URI.

FileVisitor

An interface for visiting files.

WatchService

An interface for watching varies file-system events such as create, delete, modify.

A quick word on Watching

To watch a directory you would register a Path object with the WatchService, as follows:

```java
import static java.nio.file.StandardWatchEventKinds.*;
// later on in some method...
Path path = Paths.get("/usr/local");
WatchService watchService = FileSystems.getDefault().newWatchService();
WatchKey watchKey = path.register(watchService, ENTRY_CREATE);
```

JVM Benefits

Java 7 adds some new features to the JVM, the language, and the runtime libraries.

The JVM has the following new features:

- Serviceability features (JRockit/hotspot convergence)
  - Java Mission Control (monitor, manage, profile)
  - Java Flight Recorder (profiling, problem analysis, debugging) (in progress)
- jdk introspection
  - jcmd - list running java processes
  - jcmd <pid> GC.class_histogram - size of classes
- Better garbage collection.

Performance Benefits

There are also Performance Benefits in the JVM and runtime libraries:

- Runtime compiler improvements.
- Sockets Direct Protocol (SDP)
- Java Class Libraries

- – Avoid contention in Date: changed from HashTable to ConcurrentHashMap
- – BigDecimal improvements (CR 7013110)
- Crypto config. files updates, CR 7036252
  - – User land crypto for SPARC T4
  - – Adler32 & CRC32 on T-series
- String(byte[], string) and String.getBytes(String) 2-3x performance.
- HotSpot JVM
  - – updated native compilers -XX:+UseNUMA on Java 7 (Linux kernel 2.6.19 or later; glibc 2.6.1).
  - – Partial PermGen removal (full removal in JDK 8) -interned String moved to Java heap.
  - – Default Hashtable table size is 1009 increase size if needed -XX:StringTableSize=n
  - – Distinct class names: XX:+UnlockExperimentalVMOptions -XX:PredictedClassLoadCount=#
- Client library updates (Nimbus Look&Feel; JLayer; translucent windows, Optimized 2d rendering)
- JDBC 4.1 updates (allow Connection, ResultSet, and Statement objects be used in try-with-resources statement)
- JAXP 1.4.5 (Parsing) (bug fixes, conformance, security, performance)
- JAXB 2.2.3 (Binding)
- Asynchronous I/O in java.io for both sockes and files (uses native platform when available)
- x86 (intel) improved 14x over 5 processor releases (jdk5 jdk 6)
- JDK 7u4 faster than Java6 and JRockit.

Backwards Compatibility

There are some issues to watch out for when upgrading to Java 7 on a large project:

- More stringent bytecode verifier for Java 7 (only issue when doing bytecode modification; work-around -XX:-UseSplitVerifier)
- Order of methods return from getMethods() has changed (not guaranteed to be in declaration order)

Java's Future

Overview

Java 8 is expected to be released in March 2014. It will have parts of project Coin that are not included in Java 7, annotations on Java Types (JSR-308), a new Date and Time API (JSR-310), tight integration with JavaFX, and Project Lambda[13].

Although it is not yet officially released, you can try it out by going to Oracle's Java 8 site[14] and downloading the latest binaries. Also, there is some limited IDE support.

This book does not cover Java 8 in depth. If you would like to know more, please check out "What's New in Java 8"[15].

New Date and Time API

Java 8 will introduce a new Date/Time API that is safer, easier to read, and more comprehensive than the previous API. Java's Calendar implementation has not changed much since it was first introduced and Joda-Time[16] is widely regarded as a better replacement. Java 8's new Date/Time API is very similar to Joda-Time.

Lambda Expressions

The biggest new feature of Java 8 is language level support for *lambda expressions* (Project Lambda). A lambda expression is essentially syntactic sugar for an anonymous class with one method (whose type is inferred). However, it will have enormous implications for simplifying development.

Here's a short example of using lambdas with the Runnable interface:

---

[13]http://openjdk.java.net/projects/jdk8/features/

[14]https://jdk8.java.net/download.html

[15]https://leanpub.com/whatsnewinjava8

[16]http://www.joda.org/joda-time/

```
1   public class Hello {
2           Runnable r1 = () -> { out.println(this); };
3           Runnable r2 = () -> { out.println(toString()); };
4
5           public String toString() { return "Hello, world!"; }
6
7           public static void main(String... args) {
8                   new Hello().r1.run(); //Hello, world!
9                   new Hello().r2.run(); //Hello, world!
10          }
11  }
```

The important thing to note is both the r1 and r2 lambdas call the toString() method of the Hello class. This demonstrates the scope available to the lambda.

Of course, lambda expressions can have arguments:

```
1   Arrays.sort(strArray,
2       (String s1, String s2) -> { s2.length() - s1.length() });
```

The above lambda expression implements the Comparator interface to sort strings by length.

Method References

Since a lambda expression is basically just an anonymous class with one method, wouldn't be nice if we could refer to existing methods instead of using a lamda expression? This is exactly what we can do with method-references.

For example, imagine you frequently need to filter a list of Files based on file types. You have a set of methods for determining a file's type:

```
1   public class FileFilters {
2           public static boolean fileIsPdf(File file) {}
3           public static boolean fileIsTxt(File file) {}
4           public static boolean fileIsRtf(File file) {}
5   }
```

Whenever you want to filter a list of files, you can use a method reference as in the following example (assuming you have already defined the methods, getFiles and open):

```
1  List<File> files = new LinkedList<>(getFiles());
2
3  open(files.stream().filter(FileFilters::fileIsRtf));
```

Default Methods

In order to add the stream method (or any others) to the core Collections API, Java needed another new feature, *Default methods* (also known as Defender Methods or Virtual Extension methods). This way they could add new methods to the List interface for example without breaking all the existing implementations[17].

Default methods can be added to any interface. Like the name implies, any class that implements the interface but does not override the method will get the default implementation.

```
1  default public Stream stream() {
2          return new Stream(this);
3  }
```

Map/Reduce

Lambda expressions and Default Methods allow us to implement map/reduce in Java 8. Actually it will be already implemented for us in the standard library.

For example, imagine you want to get the current point scores from a list of player-names and find the player with the most points. You have a simple class, PlayerPoints, and a getPoints method defined as the following:

```
1   public static class PlayerPoints {
2    public final String name;
3    public final long points;
4
5    public PlayerPoints(String name, long points) {
6      this.name = name;
7      this.points = points;
8    }
9
10   public String toString() {
11     return name + ":" + points;
12   }
13  }
```

---

[17]This is referred to as "Backwards Compatibility"

```
14
15  public static long getPoints(final String name) {
16         // gets the Points for the Player
17  }
```

Finding the highest player could be done very simply in Java 8 as shown in the following code:

```
1  PlayerPoints highestPlayer =
2    names.stream().map(name -> new PlayerPoints(name, getPoints(name)))
3         .reduce(new PlayerPoints("", 0.0),
4                     (s1, s2) -> (s1.points > s2.points) ? s1 : s2);
```

This could also be done in Java 7 with the dollar library (or similarly with Guava or Functional-Java), but it would be much more verbose as shown in the following:

```
1   PlayerPoints highestPlayer =
2     $(names).map(new Function<String, PlayerPoints>() {
3                   public PlayerPoints call(String name) {
4                       return new PlayerPoints(name, getPoints(name));
5                   }
6          })
7          .reduce(new PlayerPoints("", 0.0),
8          new BiFunction<PlayerPoints, PlayerPoints, PlayerPoints>() {
9                   public PlayerPoints call(PlayerPoints s1, PlayerPoints s2) {
10                      return (s1.points > s2.points) ? s1 : s2;
11                  }
12         });
```

The major benefit to coding this way (apart from the reduction in lines of code) is the ability to hide the underlying implementation of map/reduce. For example, it's possible that map and reduce are implemented concurrently, allowing you to easily take advantage of multiple processors. We'll describe one way to do this (ParallelArray) in the following section.

Parallel Array

The ParallelArray was part of JSR-166, but ended up being excluded from the standard Java lib[18]. It does exist and was released to the public domain (you can download it from the JSR website).

Although it is already out there, it really won't become easy to use until closures are included in the Java language. In Java 7 using the ParallelArray it looks like the following:

---

[18]http://puredanger.com/tech/2009/11/15/jsr-166-concurrency-updates-hit-jdk-7/

```
1   // with this class
2   public class Student {
3       String name;
4       int graduationYear;
5       double gpa;
6   }
7   // this predicate
8   final Ops.Predicate<Student> isSenior =
9           new Ops.Predicate<>() {
10                  public boolean op(Student s) {
11                          return s.graduationYear == Student.THIS_YEAR;
12                  }
13          };
14  // and this conversion operation
15  final Ops.ObjectToDouble<Student> selectGpa =
16          new Ops.ObjectToDouble<>() {
17                  public double op(Student student) {
18                          return student.gpa;
19                  }
20          };
21  // create a fork-join-pool
22  ForkJoinPool fjPool = new ForkJoinPool();
23  ParallelArray<Student> students = new ParallelArray<>(fjPool, data);
24  // find the best GPA:
25  double bestGpa = students.withFilter(isSenior)
26                              .withMapping(selectGpa)
27                              .max();
```

In Java 8, you'll be able to do the following:

```
1   // create a fork-join-pool
2   ForkJoinPool pool = new ForkJoinPool();
3   ParallelArray<Student> students = new ParallelArray<>(pool,data);
4   // find the best GPA:
5   double bestGpa = students
6       .withFilter((Student s) -> (s.graduationYear == THIS_YEAR))
7       .withMapping((Student s) -> s.gpa)
8       .max();
```

However, Java 8's addition of *stream()* and *parallelStream()* make this even more simple:

```
1  double bestGpa = students
2      .parallelStream()
3      .filter(s -> (s.graduationYear == THIS_YEAR))
4      .map(s -> s.gpa)
5      .max();
```

This makes it extremely simple to switch between a sequential implementation and a concurrent one.

Groovy GPars

You can do something similar to this right now if you use Groovy with the GPars library in the following way:

```
1  GParsPool.withPool {
2      // a map-reduce functional style (students is a Collection)
3      def bestGpa = students.parallel
4          .filter{ s -> s.graduationYear == Student.THIS_YEAR }
5          .map{ s -> s.gpa }
6          .max()
7  }
```

The static method `GParsPool.withPool` takes in a closure and augments any Collection with several methods (using Groovy's Category mechanism). The `parallel` method actually creates a ParallelArray (JSR-166) from the given Collection and uses it with a thin wrapper around it.[a]

---

[a]http://gpars.org/1.0.0/A>guide/guide/dataParallelism.html#dataParallelism_map-reduce

Introducing Dollar

Dollar says it's a "Java API that unifies collections, arrays, iterators/iterable, and char sequences", but it's actually much more. It essentially implements many of the Collection features that will come with Java 8 in a pre-Java8 library.

Much like *jQuery*[19], it utilizes the $ symbol, which although not usually accepted by Java naming conventions, is a valid Java name and makes for concise and readable code. In addition to unifying Collections and arrays, it also adds many useful methods that you might find in other languages, like "join", "slice", "repeat", "concat", "reverse" and many others.

The following lists some example code from the dollar wiki:

---

[19]http://jquery.com/

```
 1  import static org.bitbucket.dollar.Dollar.*;
 2  // repeat a String
 3  String repeat = $("abc").repeat(3).join(" "); // "abc abc abc"
 4
 5  // convert and sort a Long[] to long[]
 6  Long[] aLongArray = { 42L, 84L };
 7  long[] longs = $(aLongArray).sort().toLongArray();
 8
 9  // fluent interface: convert a primitive int array to java.util.List
10    // in the reversed order
11  int[] array = { 4, 2, -5 };
12  List<Integer> list = $(array).sort().reverse().toList();
13
14  // you can even unbox a short[] array to long[]
15  //  (since it doesn't cause a loss of precision)
16  short[] shorts = { 42, 42, 42 };
17  long[] $(shorts).toLongArray();
18
19  // syntactic sugar
20  $("a string").size();    // "a string".length()
21  $(aCollection).size();   // aCollection.size()
22  $(anArray).size();       // anArray.length
23  $(array).toString();     // calls Arrays.toString()
24  int max = $(array).max(); // finds maximum value
```

It also has the following functionality:

1. A bunch of additional core methods: min, max, each, any, all, find, indexOf, reduce
2. Ranges (with optional step): $(begin, end)
3. Lazy filtering and mapping.
4. Simple DSL for creating random numbers.

If you wish the Java API was more consistent and more functional with arrays, lists, sets, Strings, and Dates (or you just like concise code), then you should check it out at dollar.bitbucket.org[20]. It's an open-source project (LGPL), that anyone can fork on bitbucket. It is also a great example of using JUnit Theories (which we will discuss later).

---

[20]https://dollar.bitbucket.org/

Bias

In the interest of full disclosure, although the author did not create dollar, he is now its main steward.

Guava

No discussion of modern Java development would be complete without mentioning Guava.

Google started releasing some internal Java code as open-source under the name Google Collections back in 2007[21]. Its creation and architecture were partly motivated by generics inroduced in JDK 1.5. This became much more than only collection support and was rebranded as *guava*. Guava contains a lot of extremely useful code and gives some hints into modern Java practice.

Collections

It adds a bunch of very useful Collection-related classes and interfaces:

- `Collections2` - Utility methods for filtering, tranforming, and getting all possible permutations of Collections.
- `BiMap` - A Map that goes both ways (one-to-one mapping where values can map back to keys).
- `Multimap` - A Map that can associate keys with an arbitrary number of values. Use instead of `Map<Foo, Collection<Bar>>`.
- `Multiset` - A set that also keeps tracks of the number of occurances of each element.
- `Table` - Uses a row and column as keys to values.

For every Collection type, it also has a static utility class with useful methods, for example:

- Lists: `newArrayList, asList, partition, reverse, transform`
- Sets: `newHashSet, filter, difference, union`
- Maps: `newHashMap, newTreeMap, filterKeys, filterValues, asMap`

Objects

Guava's `Objects` class contains a bunch of useful methods for dealing with a lot of the broiler-plate code in generic Java, such as writing equals and hashCode methods.

- `Objects.equal(Object, Object)` - null safe equals.
- `Objects.hashCode(Object...)` - an easy way to get a hash code based on multiple fields of your class.
- `Objects.firstNonNull(Object,Object)` - one way to deal with null-return values (returns the first non-null value).

---

[21]http://publicobject.com/2007/09/series-recap-coding-in-small-with.html

Concurrency

It also contains some concurrency support, such as the following:

ListenableFuture

A ListenableFuture allows you to register callbacks to be executed once the computation is complete, or if the computation is already complete, immediately. This simple addition makes it possible to efficiently support many operations that the basic Future interface cannot support.

```
1   ListeningExecutorService srv = MoreExecutors
2          .listeningDecorator(Executors.newFixedThreadPool(10));
3   ListenableFuture<Rocket> rocket = srv.submit(new Callable<Rocket>(){
4     public Rocket call() {
5       return launchIntoSpace();
6     }
7   });
8   Futures.addCallback(rocket, new FutureCallback<Rocket>() {
9     // we want this handler to run immediately after we launch!
10    public void onSuccess(Rocket rocket) {
11      navigateToMoon(rocket);
12    }
13    public void onFailure(Throwable thrown) {
14      launchEscapePod();
15    }
16  });
```

Functional Programming

Guava contains a lot of Functional programming paradigms. It has interfaces (Function, Predicate) and utility classes (Functions, Predicates) for dealing with functional programming in Java. However, the Guava team warns against overuse of these classes in the following from the guava wiki[22].

> Excessive use of Guava's functional programming idioms can lead to verbose, confusing, unreadable, and inefficient code. These are by far the most easily (and most commonly) abused parts of Guava, and when you go to preposterous lengths to make your code "a one-liner," the Guava team weeps.

---

[22]https://code.google.com/p/guava-libraries/wiki/FunctionalExplained#Functions_and_Predicates

Optional

Guava also has Optional[23] for avoiding null return values (which is similar to Nat Pryce's Maybe[24] class and Scala's `Option` class we will discuss later).

You can use `Optional.of(x)` to wrap a non-null value, `Optional.absent()` to represent a missing value, or `Optional.fromNullable(x)` to create an Optional from a reference that may or may not be null.

After creating an instance of Optional, you then use `isPresent()` to determine if the there is a value. Optional provides a few other helpful methods for dealing with missing values:

- `or(T)` - Returns the given default value if the Optional is empty.
- `or(Supplier<T>)` - Calls on the given Supplier to provide a value if the Optional is empty.
- `or(Optional<? extends T>)` - Useful for method-chaining; returns the given Optional if the Optional is empty.
- `orNull()` - simply unwraps the value (not recommended).
- `asSet()` - Returns a set of one element if there is a value, otherwise an empty set.

Other Useful Classes

Guava also contains tons of helpful utilities for general software development, such as the following:

EventBus

EventBus allows publish-subscribe-style communication between components without requiring the components to explicitly register with one another (and thus be aware of each other).

CacheBuilder

Builds caches that can load and evict values. Caches are tremendously useful in a wide variety of use cases. For example, you should consider using caches when a value is expensive to compute or retrieve, and you will need its value on a certain input more than once.

BloomFilter

Bloom filters are a probabilistic data structure, allowing you to test if an object is definitely not in the filter, or was probably added to the Bloom filter.

ComparisonChain

A small, easily overlooked class that's useful when you want to write a comparison method that compares multiple values in succession and should return when the first difference is found. It removes all the tedium of that, making it just a few lines of chained method calls.

---

[23]http://docs.guava-libraries.googlecode.com/git/javadoc/com/google/common/base/Optional.html

[24]http://www.natpryce.com/articles/000776.html

CharMatchers

A really fast way to match characters, such as whitespace and digits.

Throwables

Lets you do some nice things with throwables, such as `Throwables.propagate` which rethrows a throwable if it's a RuntimeException or an Error and wraps it in a RuntimeException and throws that otherwise.

Guava has great documentation available on the google-code wiki[25].

---

[25]https://code.google.com/p/guava-libraries/wiki/GuavaExplained

Maven

What is Maven?

Maven[26] is an XML based declarative project manager (generally for Java projects). Maven is used for building Java projects, but encompasses much, much more. Maven is also a set of standards that allows Java/JVM developers to easily define and integrate dependencies into large projects. Maven somewhat replaces Ant[27], but can also integrate with it and other build tools.

Maven was mostly a reaction to the huge number of open-source libraries Java projects tend to rely on. Although Maven is an Apache open-source project, it could be said that the core of Maven is *Maven Central*, a repository of open-source libraries run by *Sonatype*, the company behind Maven.

Ivy[28] is a similar build tool, but is more closely related to Ant.

Many build tools, such as Ivy and Gradle[29], build on top of Maven's concept.

Using Maven

The main file that defines a Maven project is the *POM* (Project Object Model). The POM file is written in XML and contains all of the dependencies, plugins, properties, and configuration data that is specific to the current project. The POM file is generally composed in the following way:

- Basic properties (artifactId, groupId, name, version, packaging)
- Dependencies
- Plugins

There is a Maven plugin for every major Java-based IDE out there (Eclipse, NetBeans, and IntelliJ IDEA) and they are very helpful. You can use the Maven plugin to create your project, add dependencies, and edit your POM files.

Starting a New Project

There is a simple way to create a new configuration file (pom.xml) and project folders using the `archetype:generate` command:

---

[26]http://maven.apache.org/
[27]http://ant.apache.org/index.html
[28]http://ant.apache.org/ivy/
[29]http://www.gradle.org/

```
1  mvn archetype:generate
```

That will list all the different kinds of projects you can create. Pick a number representing the type of project you want (there are 726 options right now). Then answer some questions regarding the name of your project. After that process, run the following command to build the project:

```
1  mvn package
```

If you want to use any additional third party libraries, you will have to edit the POM to include each dependency. Fortunately, most IDEs make it easy to add dependencies to the POM.

 Maven the Complete Reference

Maven the Complete Reference[30] is available online if you want to learn more.

Lifecycle

Maven uses a declarative style (unlike Ant which uses a more imperative approach). This means that instead of listing the steps to take, you describe what should happen during certain phases of the build. The main phases in Maven are as follows:

- `validate` - validate the project is correct and all necessary information is available.
- `compile` - compile the source code of the project.
- `test` - test the compiled source code using a suitable unit testing framework.
- `package` - take the compiled code and package it in its distributable format, such as a JAR.
- `integration-test` - process and deploy the package if necessary into an environment where integration tests can be run.
- `verify` - run any checks to verify the package is valid and meets quality criteria.
- `install` - install the package into the local repository, for use as a dependency in other projects locally.
- `deploy` - done in an integration or release environment, copies the final package to the remote repository for sharing with other developers and projects.

 There are more phases[31], but you don't need to know all of them until you are doing more complex builds.

---

[30]http://www.sonatype.com/books/mvnref-book/reference/

[31]https://maven.apache.org/guides/introduction/introduction-to-the-lifecycle.html#Lifecycle_Reference

Executing Code

However, sometimes you just need more control over your build. In Maven, you can execute groovy code, Ant build files, Scala code, and you can even write your own plugins in groovy.

For example, you can put groovy code in your pom file in the following way:

```xml
<plugin>
  <groupId>org.codehaus.groovy.maven</groupId>
  <artifactId>gmaven-plugin</artifactId>
  <executions>
   <execution>
      <id>groovy-magic</id>
      <phase>prepare-package</phase>
      <goals>
        <goal>execute</goal>
      </goals>
      <configuration>
        <source>
          def depFile = new File(project.build.outputDirectory, 'deps.txt')

          project.dependencies.each() {
            depFile.write("${it.groupId}:${it.artifactId}:${it.version}")
          }

          ant.copy(todir: project.build.outputDirectory ) {
            fileset(dir: project.build.sourceDirectory)
          }
        </source>
      </configuration>
    </execution>
  </executions>
</plugin>
```

The above code would write out every dependency of the project into the file deps.txt. Then it would copy all of the source files into the project.build.outputDirectory (usually target/classes).

 See chapters 2, 3, and 4 in The Maven Cookbook[32].

---

[32]http://books.sonatype.com/mcookbook/reference/index.html

Deploying to Maven Central

Maven Central is the main default repository for all open source libraries. It is possible for you to deploy artifacts to Maven Central, if you want to release some software as open-source and make it available to everyone. However, you must follow a specific set of rules (correct package names, owning the URL related to software). For example if your software is packaged under "org.groovy" you need to be the owner of the URL *groovy.org*.

The initial process of deploying to Maven Central only takes a few hours. If you're interested in deploying to Maven Central, check out the following links. When you're ready to release, you have to "Close" and then also "Release" your project.

- Official Sonatype OSS Usage Guide[33]
- Sonatype blog post[34]
- Releasing a project to Maven[35]

---

[33]https://docs.sonatype.org/display/Repository/Sonatype+OSS+Maven+Repository+Usage+Guide

[34]http://www.sonatype.com/people/2009/06/publishing-your-artifacts-to-the-central-maven-repository/

[35]http://www.jroller.com/holy/entry/releasing_a_project_to_maven

Continuous Development and Testing

"The purpose of automated testing is to enable change. Verifying correctness is just a nice side effect." - Jeremy Norris

Continuous software development (also called *Agile* or Iterative development) is extremely popular nowadays and for good reason. Automated tests (tests that run after ever commit or every night) are a very important part of practicing continuous software development. Generally, as a programmer, you should write tests to verify that your code is correct.

Testing is a huge subject, which could fill another whole book, but here we will just give a short summary of modern testing in a Java/JVM environment.

Definitions

The following are important terms and acronyms in software development:

Unit Test
> Testing a single API call or some isolated code.

Integration Tests
> Testing higher order code that requires a test harness, mocking, etc.

Continuous Integration
> Having a SCM, centralized build-system, continuous building (automated build system), and having a lot of tests (comprehensive test suite).

TDD
> Test Driven Development - writing your tests before and while you write functional code.

BDD
> Behavior-Driven Development - aims to help focus development on the delivery of prioritized, verifiable business value by providing a common vocabulary that spans the divide between Business and Technology.

Types of Testing

The following are types of test you should write:

- Acceptance tests - High level tests that match the business requirements.
- Compatibility - Make sure that things work together.
- Functional - Make sure stuff works.
- Black box - Test without knowing/thinking-about what's going on in the code.
- White box - Writing tests with the code being tested in mind.
- Gray box - Hybrid of black and white.
- Regression - Creating a test after finding a bug to make sure bug does not reappear.
- Smoke - A huge sampling of data.
- Load/Stress/Performance - Seeing how the system handles load.

Test Frameworks

There are many different test frameworks for composing and running tests. The following are some of the best testing frameworks available for Java/JVM testing:

- JUnit[36] - a programmer-oriented testing framework for Java.
- TestNG[37] - a testing framework inspired from JUnit.
- Spock[38] - a testing and specification framework for Java and Groovy applications.
- JBehave[39] - a framework for BDD in Java.
- easyb[40] - another framework for BDD with a Groovy DSL.
- Arquillian[41] - a component model for your integration testing.

 We will cover JUnit and Spock in subsequent chapters.

When evaluating test frameworks, the following features should be kept in mind:

- Tests should be portable to any supported container.

---

[36]http://junit.org/

[37]http://testng.org/doc/

[38]https://code.google.com/p/spock/

[39]http://jbehave.org/

[40]http://easyb.org/

[41]http://arquillian.org/

- Tests should be executable from both IDE and build tool.
- Tests should be easy to read and understand.

Mocking interfaces and classes goes hand-and-hand with writing tests, but there are different frameworks available for mocking. The following are some great mocking frameworks:

- EasyMock[42]
- Mockito[43]
- JMock[44]

Arquillian

Arquillian[45] is a component model for your integration testing.

- Integrates with existing test frameworks.
- Creates a deployment of an application for your test: `@Deployment`
- You can use a yaml file with test data for your mock-database: `@UsingDataSet("test_-objects.yml")`
- Fragments within a page can be found and used in the test: `@FindBy(id or xpath)`
- `Warp.execute(ClientAction)` to execute an action and verify the results.

Automated Build Systems

To run your tests every night, or after every commit, you need a build system (or *continuous integration server*). The most popular Java build systems are as follows:

- Jenkins[46] - open-source community project, licensed under MIT License.
- Hudson[47] - official Oracle project, now hosted partly as an Eclipse Foundation project.
- Bamboo[48] - commercial product by Atlassian.

---

[42]http://easymock.org/

[43]http://www.mockito.org/

[44]http://www.jmock.org/

[45]http://arquillian.org/

[46]http://jenkins-ci.org/

[47]http://www.hudson-ci.org/

[48]https://www.atlassian.com/software/bamboo/overview

JUnit

What is JUnit?

JUnit[49] is a simple framework to write repeatable tests.

A typical JUnit 4.x test consists of multiple methods annotated with the @Test annotation.

At the top of every JUnit test class you should include all the static Assert methods, and annotations, like so:

```
1   import static org.junit.Assert.*;
2   import org.junit.Test;
3   import org.junit.Before;
4   import org.junit.After;
```

Use the @Before to annotate initialization methods that are run before every test and @After to annotate break-down methods that are run after every test.

Each test method should test one thing, and the method-name should reflect the purpose of the test. For example:

```
1   @Test
2   public void toStringYieldsTheStringRepresentation() {
3           String[] array = {"a", "b", "c"};
4           ArrayWrapper<String> arrayWrapper = new ArrayWrapper<String>(array);
5           assertEquals("[a, b, c]", arrayWrapper.toString());
6   }
```

Hamcrest

In more recent versions (JUnit 4.4+[50]) JUnit also includes Hamcrest matchers:

---

[49]http://junit.org/
[50]http://junit.sourceforge.net/doc/ReleaseNotes4.4.html

```
1  import static org.hamcrest.Matchers.*;
2  import static org.junit.Assert.*;
```

Then you can create more readable tests using the Hamcrest core-matchers. For example:

```
1  @Test
2  public void sizeIs10() {
3          assertThat(wrapper.size(), is(10));
4  }
```

Assumptions

Many times there are variables outside of a test that are beyond your control, but that your test assumes to be true. When an assumption fails, it shouldn't necessarily mean your test fails. For this purpose, JUnit added `assumeThat`, which you may import like so:

```
1  import static org.junit.Assume.*;
```

Then, you can verify assumptions before your assertions in your tests. For example:

```
1  assumeThat(File.separatorChar, is('/'));
```

When an assumption fails, the test is either marked as passing or ignored, depending on the version of JUnit[51].

The Beauty of JUnit Theories

JUnit theories[52] are included in JUnit[53]4.5 and above.

JUnit theories allow you to easily test code using multiple data points. Much like the name suggests it treats code as "theory" that you are trying to prove. You can also reuse the same data points for multiple test methods.

If you have multiple methods annotated with `@Theory`, each of these methods will be called *for each data-point*. This has enormous power. You may tend to hate writing tests generally, but with theories, writing tests feels so much more effective.

You can use the following annotations to configure your theories:

---

[51]http://junit.sourceforge.net/doc/ReleaseNotes4.4.html
[52]https://blogs.oracle.com/jacobc/entry/junit_theories
[53]http://www.junit.org/

- @Theory - annotates the test methods (instead of @Test).
- @RunWith(Theories.class) - annotate the class to use JUnit theories.
- @DataPoint - annotates a public static single data-point.
- @DataPoints - annotates a public static method (or field) of multiple data-points as an array.

The following example tests multiple implementations of the List interface:

```java
1  import static org.junit.Assert.*;
2  import java.util.*;
3  import org.junit.experimental.theories.*;
4  import org.junit.runner.RunWith;
5
6  @RunWith(Theories.class)
7  public class ListTest {
8
9      @DataPoint
10     public static List arrayList = new ArrayList();
11
12     @DataPoint
13     public static List linkedList = new LinkedList();
14
15     @Theory
16     public void addingElementsIncreasesSize(List list) {
17         int sizeBefore = list.size();
18         list.add(new Object());
19         int sizeAfter = list.size();
20         assertEquals("size should increase by 1",
21                 sizeBefore + 1, sizeAfter);
22     }
23 }
```

If you want to test different combinations of multiple values, you can even use the *Cartesian product*[54] of multiple data-points (all possible well-typed combinations of data-points). For example, the following test will produce 3*3 = 9 lines of output.

---

[54]https://en.wikipedia.org/wiki/Cartesian_product

```
1   @RunWith(Theories.class)
2   public class DataPointCombinationsTest {
3       @DataPoints public static int[] xData = new int[] {1, 2, 3};
4       @DataPoints public static long[] yData = new long[] {4, 5, 6};
5
6       @Theory
7       public void shouldPrint(int x, long y) {
8             System.out.println("x, y : " + x + ", " + y);
9       }
10  }
```

This will work with any number of parameters. For example, the following would produce 3*2*2 = 12 lines of output.

```
1   @RunWith(Theories.class)
2   public class DataPointCombinationsTest2 {
3       @DataPoints public static Integer[] xData = new Integer[] {1, 2, 3};
4       @DataPoints public static Long[] yData = new Long[] {42, 52};
5       @DataPoints public static String[] sData = new String[] {"Y", "N"};
6
7       @Theory
8       public void shouldPrint(Integer num, Long id, String yes) {
9             System.out.println("num, id, yes : " + num + ", " + id + ", " + yes);
10      }
11  }
```

This is what makes JUnit Theories a very powerful (and beautiful) way to test.

Concurrency in Java

As discussed earlier, multi-core processors will become standard in the future. For this reason, it's very important to know how to do concurrent programming.

State of Concurrent Programming in Java

Java doesn't have great support for concurrency built-in. Other languages, like Scala and Clojure, have been built from the ground-up with concurrency in mind. However, we can use the concurrency models from Scala and Clojure straight in Java.

Prominent Models for Concurrency

- Synchronize and suffer (using `synchronize` keyword in Java).
- Futures and the `ExecutorService`
- Software Transactional Memory (STM) (Clojure).
- Actor based model (akka).

Synchronize in Java

The original style of concurrent programming in Java involves using the `synchronize` keyword whenever shared resources are modified. The runtime behavior of this style of programming is very unpredictable and difficult to test. You must deal with the following problems:

- No warnings or errors are given at compile-time.
- Dead-locks can occur if you're not careful.
- It's very difficult to make sure you've done everything right, and errors can occur randomly.

In conclusion, the `synchronize` keyword is too low level to use (just don't use it!).

Java Futures

You may have heard of the java.util.concurrent.Future[55] interface in Java. Maybe you've even used it.

This interface was added in Java 1.5 and it holds the result of an asynchronous computation. It contains methods to check if the asynchronous computataion is complete or still in progress, to wait for the completion of the computation, and to block the call until the completion of the computation, and to retrieve the result of the computation.

Oracle plans to replace the Future interface at some point with something better (they do not specify when this will happen).

There are tons of problems with this interface:

- When using Java's Future, we tend to loop on isDone(), which ties up the thread, or call get() which blocks the thread completely.
- ExecutorService#submit(x) is used the most, (which returns a Future with a `get()` method that returns null).
  - Generally when "going asychronous" we don't care about the result, or we want to do something with the result (thus we want something like a continuation).
  - We need a callback - removes the need for polling (isDone) and blocking. (Guava's ListenableFuture provides this.)
  - Asynchronous methods should always return void.

For these reasons, if you do any concurrent programming, you should use the new Java 7 concurrency API, (ForkJoinPool and ForkJoinTask) or another concurrency framework.

STM in Clojure

STM results in a separation of State and Identity. For example, the stock price at a given time is immutable. You must use a "Transaction" to modify anything.

We can include the Clojure jars and use them within Java. For example, in the following code `referenceToAmount` can only be modified inside of a Transaction:

---

[55]http://docs.oracle.com/javase/6/docs/api/java/util/concurrent/Future.html

```
1    import clojure.lang.*
2    Ref referenceToAmount;
3    LockingTransaction.runInTransaction(new Callable() {
4            referenceToAmount.set(value);
5    });
```

Now you will get an error if you try to modify the Ref outside of a Transaction. This makes concurrent programming easier because modifying data outside of a synchronize block is impossible.

Actors

The Scala-based actor framework *Akka* can also be used from Java. Akka is also used by the Play framework[56], which will be discussed later.

The following code shows a simple example using the Akka framework with one actor:

```
1    import akka.actor.*
2    public class XActor extends UntypedActor {
3      public void onReceive(Object message) throws Exception {
4            if (message instanceof String)
5              System.out.println((String) message);
6      }
7    }
8    public static void main(String... args) {
9            ActorSystem system = ActorSystem.create("MySystem");
10           ActorRef actor = system.actorOf(new Props(XActor.class), "actor");
11           // the message could be anything implementing Serializable
12           actor.tell("Message String");
13    }
```

An actor runs in a dedicated Thread, so it can only do one thing at a time. This makes concurrency much easier to implement.

Groovy GPars

It's worth noting that the Actor and STM concurrency patterns are not limited to Scala and Clojure. Groovy's GPars[57] library implements these patterns as well and is also usable from Java. It also has DSL's that wrap the new JSR-166 features of Java, such as the Fork-Join framework, making them easier to use.

Its ParallelArray DSL was covered in the chapter on Java 8.

---

[56]http://www.playframework.org/

[57]http://gpars.codehaus.org/

Part II: JVM Languages

Other JVM Languages

Since the JVM runs Java byte-code, not actual Java-code, it is possible to compile different languages into byte-code to be run on the JVM. Also, some languages, like Groovy, are interpreted at runtime on top of the JVM.

Why use non-Java Languages?

There are many different reasons to use other languages on the JVM. You're able to quickly change code in production or development and not have to recompile your codebase. This can make development faster and more flexible. Also, other languages have features that Java does not have that can increase developer productivity and make new things possible (such as closures, mixins, and meta-programming). Although these languages are completely different from Java, they still run on the JVM and can interoperate with Java-based libraries.

The trade-off when using these other languages tends to be performance. However, the value of developer time gained is generally much more than the cost of the performance lost. In addition, Java 7 has added some features to the JVM to enhance the performance of dynamic languages (invokedynamic[58]).

Here's a table of some popular JVM languages compared with features of Java.

	Java	Groovy	Scala	Clojure
Typed?	Static	Either	Static	Dynamic
Closures?	No	Yes	Yes	Yes
Mixins?	No	Yes	Yes	Yes
Meta-programming?	No	Yes	Yes	Yes

Scala is a very concise and flexible language with both functional and object-oriented features. It has Type inference to make it very concise and Traits for multiple-inheritance (or *mixins*). It has *implicits* for meta-programming.

Groovy is very similar in syntax to Java, but with closures, dynamic typing, meta-programming (via metaClass) and many other things added. Java code is generally valid Groovy code. Groovy is interpreted at runtime, but in Groovy 2.0 the ability to compile to byte-code and enforce type-checking were added to the language.

Clojure is a reboot of Lisp on the JVM, with its macro system and code-as-data philosophy. If you're not familiar with Lisp, its syntax is very different from other languages, but it can be very powerful

---

[58]http://docs.oracle.com/javase/7/docs/technotes/guides/vm/multiple-language-support.html

when used by a skilled programmer.

Polyglot Programming

Of course, the great thing about programming today is that you don't need to strictly limit yourself to one language. You can "use the right tool for the job" every time and become a *polyglot programmer*.

Choosing a language is an important consideration whenever you start a new project. There are strong opinions on all sides of this issue, but you need to make your own decision. When making the decision of which programming language to use, consider the following:

- How many junior level people will be modifying the code?
- Is everyone on the team familiar with this language?
- Is this project more like scripting, or more like business logic?

If there are lots of junior developers or the project is business logic, you may want to stick to a statically typed language.

Dynamic Languages, Refactoring IDE, pick one...

Dynamic languages, like *Groovy, Ruby, and Javascript*, cannot support automatic refactoring like statically-typed languages do (ie. Java and Scala), since there is no way to determine everywhere a method is called for example. For some, this is a deal breaker.

Refactoring

Refactoring means changing the code in a way that does not effect functionality. It is only meant to make the code easier to understand or to prepare for some future addition of functionality (sometimes just to make something easier to test). The following actions are refactorings:

- Changing a method or class name (renaming).
- Moving a class from an anonymous class to a top level class.
- Moving a method from one class to another.
- Moving a field from one class to another.
- Creating a new class using a set of methods and fields from a class.
- Changing a local variable to become a class field.
- Replacing a bunch of literals (strings or numbers) with a constant (static final).

Edge-Craft

The concept of *Edge-craft* comes from Seth Godin's book, "Free Prize Inside"[59]. It's a way of brainstorming to come up with new, remarkable ideas. This applies not only to products and services, but anything new that you'd like to sell or give away.

In a nutshell, Edge-craft means finding a conceptual "edge" and getting as close to it as your "customers" would dare you to go. For example, Seth Godin sold his book in a cereal box. Another example: the Hummer dared to be the biggest SUV ever.

In contrast, big companies tend to sell products that appeal to the biggest market possible, and so tend to have bland products. This might be why Microsoft has been in decline. Who's the target market of Windows? Everyone. Of course, they've been very successful for a long time, as has Java. But after the popularity of Apple's iPod and iPhone, Windows became at risk of losing market share.

Java (the language) is much the same way today. It's target market is mobile (Java ME, Android), server-side, desktop-computers, household-appliances, ..., everything! Not to say this is a bad thing. The ubiquity of Java is evidence it has been extremely successful at widespread adoption. However, from a marketing stand-point, it's difficult to pin down what Java does best. Is it a mobile/embedded language? Is it a scalable server-side language? It has no edge because it has *every* edge.

In contrast, look at Ruby. When you think of Ruby, what comes to mind? Mainly, Ruby-on-Rails (RoR), a server-side web-application oriented framework.

Of course, no one did this on purpose. The history of Ruby is one of chaos. One programmer decided to write RoR in Ruby, lot's of people liked it, and it blossomed into what it is today.

Java has slowly evolved over the past decade, and many say it hasn't moved fast enough. This has caused many developers to jump ship and move to more dynamic or functional languages like Ruby, Scala, Clojure, Groovy, and Javascript (with Node.js). Java 8[60] will finally add closures (known as Project Lambda), but for some it will be too little, too late.

Now, Java the language is completely separate from the JVM, which as of Java 7, has been modified to be even better at running dynamic languages (like Ruby, Scala, and Groovy) on top of it. So, as a Java developer, there is less of a reason to stick to only Java code. We can still use Java for what it does best, and migrate to other languages for what they do best.

Java.next(): Groovy vs. Scala

Groovy seems like a natural step forward for Java developers, especially with the Grails framework. With the strong support of SpringSource[61], Groovy and Grails should continue to be successful, but it seems to be growing very slowly compared to other languages. Besides Grails, Groovy has a large ecosystem which bodes well for its future.

---

[59]http://www.sethgodin.com/freeprize/

[60]http://jdk8.java.net/

[61]http://www.springsource.org/

Scala is also a strong contender for Java developers. It has grown in popularity very quickly over the past few years and has strong support from TypeSafe[62] with their "Scala, Akka, Play" stack.

Adoption

Although not the only measure, adoption is an important measure since the more widely adopted a language is, the more jobs will be available with it, and the better its ecosystem will be.

A great way to find out about language adoption is Ohloh[63]. As you can see (if you follow that link), Scala overcame Groovy around 2010, but really took off in 2012.

Performance

Performance is another important issue with languages. However, this can change very quickly as language developers or the JVM improves over time. Also, for most projects, runtime performance is not the biggest priority. Developer-time is often a higher priority so the ease-of-use and ecosystem of the language is important.

If performance is a big issue, you'd probably choose Scala, although Groovy 2.0 now has optional static-compilation and so its performance can be close to Java[64]. However, in real-life, performance is greatly effected by what framework and/or libraries you use and how *easy* (or hard) they make it to be performant.

Web Frameworks

Especially now with the introduction of the Play framework 2.0[65], Scala is looking like a huge contender in the "highly-scalable" web world. Scala proponents claim it makes things like multi-threading and error handling, and thus scaling, easier[66], while still making small projects a breeze.

Grails 2.0 has introduced some compelling features for scalability as well. For example, it supports the Servlet 3.0 async features[67], has a `@Cachable` annotation, supports NoSQL back-ends (like MongoDB), and has plugins for automatically gzipping and caching resources.

Wouldn't it be nice if someone did a head-to-head comparison of Grails and Play? It turns out Matt Raible and James Ward did just that[68]. The main difference between the two comes from their differing goals. Grails was built to get up-and-running fast with a database-driven web-application and provide a huge ecosystem of plugins to speed-up development. Play's primary goal is to create highly-scalable web-applications, so it puts more emphasis on the asynchronous framework (akka). Also, Scala is statically typed, whereas Groovy is not by default.

---

[62]http://typesafe.com/

[63]https://www.ohloh.net/languages/compare?commit=Update&l0=groovy&l1=scala&l2=clojure&l4=-1&measure=contributors&percent=true

[64]http://java.dzone.com/articles/groovy-20-performance-compared

[65]http://blog.typesafe.com/introducing-play-20

[66]https://jazzy.id.au/default/2012/11/02/scaling_scala_vs_java.html

[67]http://burtbeckwith.com/blog/?p=1251

[68]http://raibledesigns.com/rd/entry/play_vs_grails_smackdown_at

Conclusion

As a Java developer you should spend time learning and using both of these languages. While Scala appears to have the performance, type-safety, and scalability edge, Groovy is easier to learn, has a big ecosystem, and is in many ways more similar to Java (and with Groovy 2.0 it now has `@StaticCompile` and `@TypeChecked`).

Groovy

What is Groovy?

Groovy is an open-source, dynamic language built for the JVM with a Java-like syntax. Although its original developer abandoned it, it was quickly taken on by Guillaume LaForge[69] who now works for SpringSource[70], a division of VMware, which supports the development of Groovy.

Groovy is very similar in syntax to Java so it is generally easy for Java developers to learn (Java code is generally valid Groovy code). However, Groovy has many additional features and relaxed syntax rules: closures, dynamic typing, meta-programming (via metaClass), semicolons are optional, regex-support, operator overloading, GStrings, and more. Groovy is interpreted at runtime, but in Groovy 2.0 the ability to compile to byte-code and enforce type-checking were added to the language.

Compact Syntax

Groovy's syntax can be made far more compact than Java. For example, the following code in Standard Java 5+:

```
1   for (String it : new String[] {"Rod", "Carlos", "Chris"})
2         if (it.length() <= 4)
3               System.out.println(it);
```

can be expressed in Groovy in one line as:

```
1   ["Rod", "Carlos", "Chris"].findAll{it.size() <= 4}.each{println it}
```

It has tons of built-in features to make the above possible (compact List definition, extensions to JDK objects, closures, optional semi-colons, and the println method, optional parenthesis).

List and Map Definitions

Groovy makes List and Map definitions much more concise and simple. You simple use brackets ([]) and the mapping (:) symbol for mapping keys to values:

---

[69]http://skillsmatter.com/expert-profile/java-jee/guillaume-laforge
[70]http://www.springsource.org/

```
1  def list = [1, 2]
2  def map = ['cars' : 2, 'boats' : 3]
3  println list.getClass() // java.util.ArrayList
4  println map.getClass() // java.util.LinkedHashMap
```

When working with maps with String keys, Groovy makes life much easier by allowing you to refer to keys using dot-notation (avoiding the get and put methods). For example:

```
1  map.cars = 2
2  map.boats = 3
3  map.planes = 0
4  println map.cars // 2
```

This even makes it possible to Mock objects using a Map when testing.

Easy Properties

Groovy takes the idea of Java Beans to a whole new level. You can get and set bean properties using dot-notation (and Groovy automatically adds getters and setters to your classes if you don't).

For example, instead of `person.getFirstName()` you can use `person.firstName`. When setting properties, instead of `person.setFirstName("Bob")` you can just use `person.firstName = 'Bob'`.

GString

Groovy adds its own class, called `GString`, that allows you to embed groovy code within strings. This is another features that makes Groovy very concise and easy to read.

For example, it makes it easy to embed a bunch of variables into a string:

```
1  def os = 'Linux'
2  def cores = 2
3  println("Cores: $cores, OS: $os, Time: ${new Date()}")
```

The dollar $ allows you to refer directly to variables, and ${code} allows you to execute arbitrary Groovy code.

 ## String

If you just want to use a `java.lang.String`, you should use single quotes ('foo').

Closures

A closure is block of code in Groovy, which may or may not take parameters and return a value. It is very similar to lambda expressions in Java 8. For example, in the above code {it.size() <= 4} and {println it} are closures.

Groovy closures have several implicit variables:

- it - If the closure has one argument, it can be referred to implicitly as **it**
- this - Refers to the enclosing class.
- owner - The same as this unless it is enclosed in another closure.
- delegate - Usually the same as owner but you can change it (this allows the methods of *delegate* to be in scope).

Closures can be passed as method arguments. When this is done (*and it is the last argument*), it may go outside the parentheses. For example:

```
1  def list = ['foo','bar']
2  def newList = []
3  list.collect( newList ) {
4    it.toUpperCase()
5  }
6  println newList // ["FOO", "BAR"]
```

 ### Return Optional

The return keyword is completely optional in Groovy. A method or closure simply returns its last expression.

A Better Switch

Groovy's switch statement is much like Java's, except that it allows many more case expressions. For example, it allows Strings, lists, ranges, and class types:

```
1   switch ( x ) {
2   case "foo":
3       result = "found foo"
4           break
5
6   case [4, 5, 6]:
7       result = "4 5 or 6"
8       break
9
10  case 12..30: // Range
11      result = "12 to 30"
12      break
13
14  case Integer:
15      result = "was integer"
16      break
17
18  case Number:
19      result = "was number"
20      break
21
22  default:
23      result = "default"
24  }
```

Gotcha's

Because Groovy is very similar to Java, but not Java, it's easy to get confused by their differences. A couple of these confusions are *boolean-resolution* and the *Map syntax sugar*.

Groovy is much more liberal in what it accepts in a boolean expression. For example, the empty-string and zero are considered `false`. So, the following prints out "true" four times:

```
1   if ("foo") println("true")
2   if (!"") println("true")
3   if (42) println("true")
4   if (! 0) println("true")
```

Groovy syntax-sugar for Maps allows you use String keys directly, which is often very helpful. However, this can cause confusion when attempting to get the class-type of a map using Groovy's property-accessor syntax sugar (`.class` refers to the key-value, not `getClass()`). So you should use the `getClass()` method directly.

Groovy 1.8

- Command Chains: `pull request on github => pull(request).on(github)`
- GPars [71]is bundled for parallel and concurrent paradigms.
- Closure annotation parameters: `@Invariant({number >= 0})`
- Closure memoization: `{...}.memoize()`
- Built-in JSON support - consuming, producing, pretty-printing
- New AST Transformations: `@Log, @Field, @AutoClone, @AutoExternalizable, ...`

Groovy 2.0

- More modular - multiple jars - create your own module (Extension modules[72])
- `@StaticCompile` - compiles your Groovy code to byte-code.
- `@TypeChecked` - enforces compile time type-checking.
- Java 7 alignments - project Coin & invoke dynamic.
- Java 7 - `catch (Exception1 | Exception2 e) {}`

Static Type Checking

If you add the `@TypeChecked` annotation to your class, it causes the compiler to enforce compile time type-checking. It will infer types for you, so your code can still be *Groovy*.

- Infers Lowest Upper Bound (LUB)
- Gotcha's:
    - Runtime meta-programming won't work!
    - Explicit type needed in closure: `a.collect {String it -> it.toUpperCase()}`

If you add the `@StaticCompile` annotation to your class, it causes the compiler to compile your Groovy code to byte-code.

- Type-checking: no one else can change byte-code.
- Binary identical to compiled Java (almost).

---

[71]http://gpars.codehaus.org/
[72]http://groovy.codehaus.org/Creating+an+extension+module

Design Patterns in Groovy

Design patterns are a great way to make your code functional, readable, and extensible. There are some patterns that are easier and require less code in Groovy compared to Java.

Strategy Pattern

Imagine you have three different methods for finding totals:

```
def totalPricesLessThan10(prices) {
        int total = 0
        for (int price : prices)
                if (price < 10) total += price
        total
}
def totalPricesMoreThan10(prices) {
        int total = 0
        for (int price : prices)
                if (price > 10) total += price
        total
}
def totalPrices(prices) {
        int total = 0
        for (int price : prices)
                total += price
        total
}
```

A lot of code is duplicated in this case. There's only one small thing that changes for each of these methods. In Groovy you can use a closure parameter instead of three different methods so you can have the following:

```
1  def totalPrices(prices, selector) {
2          int total = 0
3          for (int price : prices)
4                  if (selector(price)) total += price
5          total
6  }
```

Now you have a method, totalPrices(prices, selector) where selector is a closure. Also, you can put the closure outside of the method parameters in a method call if it's the last parameter. So you can call the above method three different ways to achieve the desired results:

```
1  totalPrices(prices) { it < 10 }
2  totalPrices(prices) { it > 10 }
3  totalPrices(prices) { true }
```

This not only makes your code more concise, it's also easier to read and extend.

Iterators

The Iterator pattern is built-in to Groovy. Every object is iterable in Groovy. This is most commonly useful for Collections, such as a List, but every object has the following methods:

- each - Typical iteration.
- eachWithIndex - Typical iteration with an index.
- collect - Iterator that builds a collection (equivalent of Scala's map)
- find - Finds the first element that matches a closure.
- findIndexOf - Finds the first element that matches a closure and returns its index.
- findAll - Finds all elements that match a closure (similar to filter in Scala).
- any - True if any element returns true for the closure.
- every - True if all elements return true for the closure.
- inject(startValue) - Loops through the values and returns a single value (equivalent of foldRight in Scala).

For example, collect makes it very simple to perform an operation on a list values:

```
1   def list = ['foo','bar']
2   def newList = []
3   list.collect( newList ) { it.substring(1) }
4   println newList //  [oo, ar]
```

DSL's

Groovy has many features that make it great for writing DSL's (Domain Specific Languages):

- Closures with delegates
- Parenthesis and dots (.) are optional
- Ability to add methods to standard classes using Category and Mixin transformations.
- The ability to override many operators (plus, minus, etc.)

Within Groovy you can take a block of code (a closure) as a parameter and then call it using a local variable as a delegate. For example, imagine you have the following code for sending SMS texts:

```
1   class SMS {
2           def from(String fromNumber) {
3                   // set the from
4           }
5           def to(String toNumber) {
6                   // set the to
7           }
8           def body(String body) {
9                   // set the body of text
10          }
11          def send() {
12                  // send the text.
13          }
14  }
```

In Java, you'd need to use this the following way:

```
1   SMS m = new SMS();
2   m.from("555-432-1234");
3   m.to("555-678-4321");
4   m.body("Hey there!");
5   m.send();
```

In Groovy you can add the following static method to the SMS class for DSL-like usage:

```
1  def static send(block) {
2          SMS m = new SMS()
3          block.delegate = m
4          block()
5          m.send()
6  }
```

This sets the SMS object as a delegate for the block so that methods are forwarded to it. With this you can now do the following:

```
1  SMS.send {
2          from '555-432-1234'
3          to '555-678-4321'
4          body 'Hey there!'
5  }
```

This removes a lot of repetition from the code.

Meta-programming

In Groovy you can add methods to classes at runtime - even to core Java libraries. For example, the following code adding the yell method to the String class:

```
1  String.metaClass.yell = { -> toUpperCase() }
```

or for a single instance:

```
1  str.metaClass.yell = { -> toUpperCase() }
```

Command pattern

In Groovy you can intercept missing methods using the methodMissing method as follows:

```
1  def methodMissing(String name, args)
```

Next you can intercept, cache and invoke the called method (GORM in Grails uses this for its query functions). For example:

```
1  def methodMissing(String name, args) {
2          impl = { /* your code */ }
3          getMetaClass()."$name" = impl
4          impl()
5  }
```

This implements the missing functionality and then adds it to the current class's metaClass so that future calls go directly to the implementation instead of the methodMissing method.

Delegation

Delegation is when a class has methods that directly call (method signature identical) methods of another class. This is hard in Java because it is difficult and time consuming to add methods to a class.

This is much easier with the new @Delegate annotation in Groovy 2.0. It's like compile-time meta-programming. It automatically adds the methods of the delegate class to the current class.

For example:

```
1  public class Person {
2          def eatDonuts() { println("yummy") }
3  }
4
5  public class RoboCop {
6          @Delegate final Person person
7
8          public RoboCop(Person person) { this.person = person }
9          public RoboCop() { this.person = new Person() }
10
11         def crushCars() {
12                 println("smash")
13         }
14 }
```

Although RoboCop does not have an eatDonuts() method, all of the methods of Person are added to RoboCop and delegated to person. This allows for the following usage:

```
1  def person = new RoboCop()
2  person.eatDonuts()
3  person.crushCars()
```

The Groovy Ecosystem

There are many different frameworks built on top of Groovy that make up the Groovy ecosystem.

Web and UI Frameworks

Grails[73]

Web-framework inspired by Ruby-on-Rails; used by Walmart's Music Store; has at least 800 plugins.

Griffon [74]

Swing UI, command-line very similar to grails: `create-app cool -archetype=jumpstart`

vert.x[75]

A framework for asynchronous application development. Not strictly a Groovy project but you can use it. It's currently an Eclipse Foundation project[76].

Cloud Computing Frameworks

Gaelyk [77]

abstraction over GAE (Google App Engine); has an emerging plugin system.

Caelyf[78]

since 2011, Apache 2 licensed framework for CloudFoundry; similar to gaelyk.

Build Frameworks

Gradle[79]

A Groovy DSL for building projects. Uses `build.gradle`.

Gant

Like Ant in Groovy. Since 2006; now in maintenance mode. Used by Grails & Griffon.

---

[73]http://grails.org/

[74]http://griffon.codehaus.org/

[75]http://vertx.io/

[76]https://groups.google.com/forum/?fromgroups=#!topic/vertx/3O6NCDQQdUU

[77]http://gaelyk.appspot.com/

[78]http://caelyf.cloudfoundry.com/

[79]http://www.gradle.org/

Testing Frameworks/Code Analysis

Easyb[80]

  BDD - behaviour driven development, human readable.

Spock[81]

  DSL testing framework. Around since 2007. Uses strings as method names. You can use datatables for test input. `@Unroll(String)` - works like JUnit theories "unrolled".

Codenarc[82]

  Static code analysis for Groovy. Around since 2009. Has plugins for Grails and Griffon.

Concurrency

GPars[83]

  A multi-threading framework for Groovy. It has a fork/join abstraction, actors, STM, and more.

Honorable Mentions

gvm[84]

  the Groovy enVironment Manager (GVM); very cool.

Ratpack[85]

  A toolkit for web applications on the JVM; and RESTful web-services.

GContracts[86]

  `@Requires, @Ensures`

---

[80]http://easyb.org/

[81]http://code.google.com/p/spock/

[82]http://codenarc.sourceforge.net/

[83]http://gpars.codehaus.org/

[84]https://github.com/gvmtool/gvm

[85]https://github.com/bleedingwolf/Ratpack

[86]http://blog.andresteingress.com/2011/03/11/gcontracts-1-2-0-released/

Gradle

Gradle is a groovy based DSL for building projects.

The Gradle website describes it as follows:

> Gradle combines the power and flexibility of Ant with the dependency management and conventions of Maven into a more effective way to build. Powered by a Groovy DSL and packed with innovation, Gradle provides a declarative way to describe all kinds of builds through sensible defaults. -gradle.org[87]

Projects and Tasks

Each Gradle build is composed of one or more projects and each project is composed of tasks.

The core of the gradle build is the `build.gradle` file (which is called the *build script*).

Tasks are defined by writing `task`, then a task-name, and then `<<` followed by a closure. For example:

```
task upper << {
        String someString = 'test'
        println "Original: $someString"
        println "Uppercase: " + someString.toUpperCase()
}
```

Tasks can contain any groovy code, but you can take advantage of existing Ant tasks; for example:

```
ant.loadfile(srcFile: file, property: 'x') //loads file into x
ant.checksum(file: file, property: "z") // put checksum into z
println ant.properties["z"] //accesses ant property z
```

The above code would load a file into ant-property "x", save the file's checksum in ant-property "z", and then print out that checksum.

---

[87]http://www.gradle.org/

Plugins

Gradle core has very little built-in, but it has powerful plugins to allow it to be very flexible.

A plugin can do one or more of the following:

- Add tasks to the project (e.g. compile, test)
- Pre-configure added tasks with useful defaults.
- Add dependency configurations to the project.
- Add new properties and methods to existing type via extensions.

We're going to concentrate on building Java-based projects, so we'll be using the java plugin (however, Gradle is not limited to Java projects!):

```
1   apply plugin: 'java'
```

This plugin uses Maven's conventions. For example, it expects to find your production source code under src/main/java and your test source code under src/test/java.

Maven Dependencies

Every Java project tends to rely on many open-source projects to be built. Gradle builds on Maven so you can easily include your dependencies using a simple DSL, like in the following example:

```
1   apply plugin: 'java'
2
3   sourceCompatibility = 1.7
4
5   repositories {
6           mavenLocal()
7           mavenCentral()
8   }
9
10  dependencies {
11          compile 'com.google.guava:guava:14.0.1'
12          compile 'org.bitbucket.dollar:dollar:1.0-beta3'
13          testCompile group: 'junit', name: 'junit', version: '4.+'
14          testCompile "org.mockito:mockito-core:1.9.5"
15  }
```

This build script uses sourceCompatibility to define the Java source code version of 1.7 (which is used during compilation). Next it tells Maven to use the local repository first (mavenLocal), then Maven Central.

In the dependencies block this build script defines two dependencies for the compile scope and two for testCompile scope. Jars in the testCompile scope are only using by tests, and won't be included in any final products.

The line for JUnit shows the more verbose style for defining dependencies.

 ## Online Documentation

Gradle has a huge online user-guide available online at gradle.org[88].

---

[88]http://www.gradle.org/docs/current/userguide/userguide.html

Spock

Spock is a testing framework for Java and Groovy applications. The Spock website[89] has this to say about Spock:

> What makes it stand out from the crowd is its beautiful and highly expressive specification language. Thanks to its JUnit runner, Spock is compatible with most IDEs, build tools, and continuous integration servers. Spock is inspired from JUnit, RSpec, jMock, Mockito, Groovy, Scala, Vulcans, and other fascinating life forms.

Introduction

The basic structure of a test class in Spock is a class that extends `Specification` and has multiple methods with Strings for names.

Spock processes the test code and allows you to use a simple groovy syntax to specify tests.

Each test is composed of labeled blocks of code with labels like "when", "then", and "where". The best way to learn Spock is with examples.

A Simple Test

Let's start by recreating a simple test from the chapter on JUnit:

```
1  def "toString yields the String representation"() {
2        def array = ['a', 'b', 'c'] as String[]
3        when:
4        def arrayWrapper = new ArrayWrapper<String>(array);
5        then:
6        arrayWrapper.toString() == '[a, b, c]'
7  }
```

As shown above, assertions are simply groovy conditional expressions. If the above "==" expression returns false, the test will fail and Spock will give a detailed printout to explain why it failed.

In the absence of any "when" clause, you can use the "expect" clause instead of "then"; for example:

---

[89]https://code.google.com/p/spock/

```
1  def "empty list size is zero"() {
2        expect: [].size() == 0
3  }
```

Mocking

Mocking interfaces is extremely easy in Spock[90]. Simply use the Mock method, as shown in the following example (where Subscriber is an interface):

```
1  class APublisher extends Specification {
2    def publisher = new Publisher()
3    def subscriber = Mock(Subscriber)
```

Now subscriber is a mocked object. You can implement methods simply using the overloaded >> operator as shown below.

```
1  def "can cope with misbehaving subscribers"() {
2      subscriber.receive(_) >> { throw new Exception() }
3
4      when:
5      publisher.send("event")
6      publisher.send("event")
7
8      then:
9      2 * subscriber.receive("event")
10 }
```

Expected behavior is described by using a number or range times (*) the method call as shown above.

The under-score (_) is treated like a wildcard (much like in Scala).

Lists or Tables of Data

Much like how JUnit has DataPoints and Theories, Spock allows you to use lists or tables of data in tests.

For example,

---

[90]You can also Mock classes, but it requires including the cglib jar as a dependency.

```
1  def "subscribers receive published events at least once"() {
2      when: publisher.send(event)
3      then: (1.._) * subscriber.receive(event)
4      where: event << ["started", "paused", "stopped"]
5  }
```

Above, the overloaded << operator is used to provide a list for the event variable. Although it is a List here, anything that is iterable could be used.

Ranges

The range 1.._ here means "one or more" times. You can also use _..3, for example, to mean "three or less" times.

Tabular formatted data can be used as well. For example:

```
1  def "length of NASA mission names"() {
2      expect:
3      name.size() == length
4
5      where:
6      name        | length
7      "Mercury"   | 7
8      "Gemini"    | 6
9      "Apollo"    | 6
10 }
```

In this case, the two columns (name and length) are used to substitute the corresponding variables in the expect block. Any number of columns can be used.

Expecting Exceptions

Use the thrown method in the then block to expect a thrown Exception.

```
1  def "peek on empty stack throws"() {
2      when: stack.peek()
3      then: thrown(EmptyStackException)
4  }
```

You can also capture the thrown exception by simply assigning it to `thrown()`. For example:

```
1  def "peek on empty stack throws"() {
2      when: stack.peek()
3      then:
4      Exception e = thrown()
5      e.toString().contains("EmptyStackException")
6  }
```

Conclusion

As you can see, Spock makes tests more concise and easy to read, and, most importantly, makes the intentions of the test clear.

Scala

What is Scala?

Scala is an open-source language that runs on the JVM. It was developed at the Programming Methods Laboratory of the Swiss Federal Institute of Technology (EPFL), mainly by Martin Odersky[91] (a co-designer of Java generics).

TypeSafe[92], a private company, offers training, commercial maintenance, support, and operations tools for Scala, as well as Akka and Play.

The Scala website has the following description of the language:

> Scala is a general purpose programming language designed to express common programming patterns in a concise, elegant, and type-safe way. It smoothly integrates features of object-oriented and functional languages, enabling Java and other programmers to be more productive. Code sizes are typically reduced by a factor of two to three when compared to an equivalent Java application. - Scala-lang.org[93]

Hello World

Here's a simple HelloWorld example in Scala:

```
1  object HelloWorld {
2    def main(args: Array[String]) {
3      println("Hello, world!")
4    }
5  }
```

You'll notice that HelloWorld is declared as an object. This is similar to the keyword static in Java, except that instead of putting the keyword on every method and field, you just wrap everything up in one block. Since the main method in Java is static, we need to put the main method in an object in Scala.

The def keyword is used to define functions.

---

[91]http://www.scala-lang.org/node/241

[92]http://typesafe.com/

[93]http://www.Scala-lang.org/

The next thing you might notice is that types are declared *after* the parameter name. In Scala type declarations always come on the right-side after a colon.

Array[String] is the equivalent of String[] in Java. Everything in Scala is an Object, including arrays.

Lastly, you'll see that the println function is called which is equivalent to System.out.println in Java.

Everything's an object

Scala has no primitives as in Java. In other words, when coding in Scala, everything is an object. However, the compiler will compile your code down to primitive math if possible, so you don't lose performance. In addition, functions are considered first-class citizens in Scala (they can be passed around as values), which is why they say Scala combines the features of object-oriented and functional languages.

To achieve this feat, everything in Scala extends from either AnyVal or AnyRef. AnyRef is the equivalent of Object in Java, but AnyVal is the super-class of all primitive values - although it appears to be an object while coding.

Defining objects in Scala is dead-simple and devoid of much of the ceremony involved in Java. Essentially, the definition of the constructor also defines the fields of the class. Combined with the fact that everything is public by default, and that the val or var keyword is used to define a field, and class definitions are very short.

For example, the following one-line class definition defines a Person class with a name and age with accessors and modifiers:

```
1   class Person(var name:String, var age:Int)
```

The keyword var means *variable*, while val (an *immutable value*) is used more frequently in the functional programming style.

Everything's an expression

Unlike in Groovy and most other languages, everything is Scala is an expression. For example, the following code snippet defines a method called eatDonuts:

```
1   def eatDonuts = println("yum")
```

Notice the lack of curly brackets.

Also, since everything is an expression, everything has a return value, replacing the need for the return keyword. For example, you might see the following method in Scala:

```
1   def toString = if (number < 0) "-" + (-number) else "+" + number
```

This also means a ternary expression (exp ? "true" : "false") would be redundant in Scala.

Match is Switch on Steroids

You can use the match statement much like a switch statement. Check out the following code for an example of the syntax:

```
1   def wordFor(number:Int) = number match {
2     case 1 => "one"
3     case 2 => "two"
4     case 3 => "three"
5     case _ => "unknown"
6   }
```

There's no need for a return or break keyword because the match statement actually returns whatever value is returned from the matched case statement.

Another thing "missing" in Scala (if your coming from Java) is the instanceof keyword and any casting. Instead, you can just use a match statement like the following:

```
1   // return a Person or null if obj is a different type.
2   var person:Person = obj match {
3     case x:Person => x
4     case _ => null
5   }
```

One of the most powerful features of matching is using *case classes*. Using case classes you are able to match values *within* a class. Let's take a look at a concrete example:

```
1   class Dimension(val width:Int, val height:Int)
2
3   case class Vertical(h:Int) extends Dimension(0, h)
4   case class Horizontal(w:Int) extends Dimension(w, 0)
5
6   def printDim(d : Dimension) = d match {
7     case Vertical(value) => println("Vert: " + value)
8     case Horizontal(value) => println("Horiz: " + value)
9
10    case dim:Dimension => {
```

```
11          print("W: " + dim.width + ", ")
12          println("H: " + dim.height)
13     }
14
15   case null => println("Invalid input")
16 }
17 printDim(Vertical(10)) //    Vert: 10
18 printDim(Horizontal(30)) // Horiz: 30
```

The above `printDim` function uses the match statement to pull out the appropriate value if the given Dimension is an instance of Vertical or Horizontal. Of course, this only works if you define the case classes, which makes them similar to Java enums, but more flexible.

> In Scala, Strings can joined by + much like in Java.

Catching Exceptions in Scala is similar to using the `match` statement. For example, see the following code where the last block is executed for all other types of exceptions:

```
1 try {...}
2 catch {
3   case e:SQLException => println("Database error")
4   case e:MalformedURLException => println("Bad URL")
5   case e => {
6         println("Some other exception type:")
7         e.printStackTrace()
8   }
9 }
```

Traits as Mixins

Scala does not have interfaces, but has Traits instead, which is somewhat like a combined Interface and Abstract-base-class in Java. However, unlike anything in Java, Traits can be applied to classes or *instances* of classes and multiple Traits can be used.

Here's an example using a Trait:

```
1  class SpaceShuttle(val name:String) {
2        def launch = println(name + " Take off!")
3  }
4  trait MoonLander {
5        def land = println("Landing!")
6  }
7  class MoonShuttle(name:String) extends SpaceShuttle(name) with MoonLander {
8  }
```

A class can "extend" any number of Traits using the with keyword. So now we can do the following:

```
1  val apollo = new MoonShuttle("Apollo 27")
2  apollo.launch
3  apollo.land
```

This would generate the following output:

```
1  Apollo 27 Take off!
2  Landing!
```

To use multiple Traits you simply add them to the end; for example:

```
1  class MoonShuttle(name:String) extends SpaceShuttle(name)
2        with MoonLander with Shuttle with Rocket
```

List and Apply

Scala's core library includes an immutable List. A list can be created very easily.

```
1  scala> val list = List(1,2,3,4)
2  list: List[Int] = List(1, 2, 3, 4)
```

Note that unlike in Java, there's no need to define the generic type of the list (Int); Scala figures this out for us.

Appending to a List has a special syntax in Scala. To append to the beginning you use :: and :+ to append to the end.

```
1  scala> 0 :: list
2  res2: List[Int] = List(0, 1, 2, 3, 4)
3
4  scala> list :+ 5
5  res3: List[Int] = List(1, 2, 3, 4, 5)
```

Note that the original list is unmodified.

The "new" keyword is unnecessary to create a List thanks to the "apply" method. Any object that has an apply method can be called with the `.apply` omitted. For example, create a Person class and companion object with the following definition:

```
1  class Person(val name:String)
2  object Person { def apply(name:String) = new Person(name) }
```

Now you can create a Person object in the following way:

```
1  scala> Person("adam")
2  res0: Person = Person@2c111e4d
3
4  scala> res0.name
5  res1: String = adam
```

Likewise, accessing a member of a list also uses the "apply" method of the list. So `list(0)` returns the first member of the list, etc.

Tuples

Scala has built-in support for Tuples. A Tuple is a typed data structure for holding a number of elements (up to 22 in Scala). Tuples are useful whenever you are handling multiple related values, but don't need all of the overhead of creating a new class.

> There are several implementations of Tuples available in Java, such as *javatuples*[a].
>
> ---
> [a]http://www.javatuples.org/

Creating a Tuple is extremely simple. For example, here's a tuple of two elements (Tuple2).

```
1  scala> var test = (42, "bitcoins")
2  test: (Int, java.lang.String) = (42,bitcoins)
3
4  scala> test._1
5  res0: Int = 42
6
7  scala> test._2
8  res1: java.lang.String = bitcoins
```

The underscore syntax works for all elements of the tuple. For example, if you have a tuple with ten elements, then _10 would refer to last element.

You can also extract elements from a tuple using the underscore "wild-card" syntax, such as:

```
1  scala> val(num, _) = test
2  num: Int = 42
```

You can also create a Tuple using the -> syntax as follows:

```
1  scala> 1 -> "a"
2  res1: (Int, java.lang.String) = (1,a)
3
4  scala> res1.getClass
5  res2: java.lang.Class[_ <: (Int, java.lang.String)] = class scala.Tuple2
```

This is so you can create maps using the following syntax:

```
1  scala> val map = Map(1 -> "a", 2 -> "b")
2  map: scala.collection.immutable.Map[Int,java.lang.String] = Map(1 -> a, 2 -> b)
```

You'll notice that the default Map implementation is immutable. Everything in Scala tends to be immutable. Although there are also mutable versions of Map, List, etc. that you can use, the functional programming paradigm that is promoted by Scala goes well with immutable data structures.

Maps

So we've learned that Maps can easily be created by calling Map() with a list of tuples, but how can you modify a Map?

Maps can be added to or removed from using the math symbols (+ and -). In the following code, "collection.immutable" was replaced with ".." for formatting reasons:

```
1   scala> val map = Map(1 -> "a")
2   map: scala....Map[Int,java.lang.String] = Map(1 -> a)
3
4   scala> map + (2 -> "B")
5   res1: scala....Map[Int,java.lang.String] = Map(1 -> a, 2 -> B)
6
7   scala> res1 - 2
8   res2: scala....Map[Int,java.lang.String] = Map(1 -> a)
9
10  scala> res1 + ((3, "C"))
11  res3: scala....Map[Int,java.lang.String] = Map(1 -> a, 2 -> B, 3 -> C)
```

 The last line above demonstrates that a key-value pair is merely a tuple.

As when adding to an immutable List, the original Map is not modified; a new Map is returned.

For Expressions

The for expression in Scala is a very powerful feature. It can used similar to a normal "for loop" but it can also be used to avoid null-pointer exceptions and for parallel programming. First we will discuss avoiding null-pointers.

To avoid null, Scala has Option[94]. Option has two implementations: Some and None. Some wrapping a value, and None representing a null value.

For example, imagine you want to create a Person object only if firstName and surname are supplied. Then using the scala command-line, define the Person class:

```
1   scala> case class Person(firstName: String, surname: String)
2   defined class Person
```

Define maybeFirstname and maybeSurname as instance of Option, with None for maybeSurname (meaning it was not supplied).

---

[94]http://www.scala-lang.org/api/current/index.html#scala.Option

```
1  scala> val maybeFirstname = Option("Adam")
2  maybeFirstname: Option[java.lang.String] = Some(Adam)
3
4  scala> val maybeSurname = Option(null)
5  maybeSurname: Option[Null] = None
```

Then, when you use the following for-comprehension, you get a None instead of null or a NullPointerException.

```
1  scala> for (firstName <- maybeFirstname; surname <- maybeSurname)
2          yield Person(firstName, surname)
3  res1: Option[Person] = None
```

Now, redefine maybeSurname with a value and rerun the for-comprehension to get the Person.

```
1  scala> val maybeSurname = Option("Davis")
2  maybeSurname: Option[java.lang.String] = Some(Davis)
3
4  scala> for (firstName <- maybeFirstname; surname <- maybeSurname)
5          yield Person(firstName, surname)
6  res2: Option[Person] = Some(Person(Adam,Davis))
```

When multiple values are assigned using <- inside a for comprehension, each value will have flatMap called on it, and the yield expression results in having map called (which results in an Option). This works because Option is iterable (like a list with one or zero elements).

This means that for expressions are particularly useful for combinatorial algorithms. For example, this combines all combinations of (1,2) and (a,b):

```
1  scala> for (x <- List(1,2); y <- List("a","b"))
2          | yield (x,y)
3  res0: List[(Int, java.lang.String)] = List((1,a), (1,b), (2,a), (2,b))
```

Note that the resulting type depends on the type of the first element. So, if x was a Set, res0 would have been a Set[(Int, String)].

For those who are interested, the equivalent to the above in Java 7 (using *javatuples*[95]) would be something like the following:

---

[95]http://www.javatuples.org/

```
1  // imports:
2  import static java.util.Arrays.asList;
3  import org.javatuples.Pair;
4  // code:
5  List<Pair<Integer,String> list = new ArrayList<>();
6  for (int x : asList(1, 2))
7          for (String y : asList("a", "b"))
8                  list.add(Pair.with(x, y));
```

For expressions can also contains filters and definitions:

```
1  for {
2          p <- persons          // a generator
3          n = p.name            // a definition
4          if (n startsWith "Foo") // a filter
5  } yield n
```

Finally, if you desire to convert your for-expression to use parallel programming, you need only add one word (as of Scala 2.9), par. Assuming persons is a collection (List or Set), the following would be executed in parallel:

```
1  for {
2          p <- persons.par
3          n = p.name
4          if (n startsWith "Foo")
5  } yield n
```

Scala 2.9

Scala 2.9 introduced some new features including:

- Parallel Collections: every collection can be converted into a corresponding parallel collection using the par method.
- App Trait: App replaces Application as a better way to write a top-level application class (args is available).
- DelayedInit Trait: If a class or object inherits from this trait, all its initialization code is packed in a closure and forwarded as an argument to a method named delayedInit which is defined as an abstract method in trait DelayedInit.
- Repl Improvements: More robust cursor handling, bash-style ctrl-R history search, new commands like :imports, :implicits, :keybindings.

- Scala Runner: `scala` can accept a jar-file, classname, or source-file as an argument.
- Java Interop:
    - The @strictfp annotation is supported.
    - Primitive types and their boxed versions are implicitly converted bidirectionally.
- New methods in collections: `collectFirst`, `maxBy`, `minBy`, `span`, `inits`, `tails`, `permutations`, `combinations`, `subsets`
- AnyRef specialization: It's possible to specialize on type parameters for subtypes of AnyRef (`class Foo[@specialize(AnyRef) T](arr: Array[T]) {...}`), which allows for more efficient array indexing and updates.

Scala 2.10

Scala 2.10 introduced a lot of new features. Some of the prominent new features include:

- Values Classes[96]: the ability to extend AnyVal.
- Implicit Classes[97]: a simplification of the definition of implicit wrappers.
- String Interpolation[98]: similar to Groovy's GString.
- Futures and Promises[99]
- Dynamic and applyDynamic[100]
- New ByteCode emitter based on ASM
- Can target JDK 1.5, 1.6 and 1.7 (Emits 1.6 bytecode by default)
- A new Pattern Matcher rewritten from scratch to generate more robust code.
- Scaladoc Improvements: Implicits (-implicits flag), Diagrams (-diagrams flag, requires graphviz), Groups (-groups)
- Modularized Language features. Get on top of the advanced Scala features used in your codebase by explicitly importing them[101].
- Parallel Collections are now configurable with custom thread pools[102].
- Akka Actors now part of the distribution (the original Scala actors are now deprecated).
- Addition of ??? and NotImplementedError
- Addition of IsTraversableOnce and IsTraversableLike type classes for extension methods.
- Some Performance Improvements (Faster inliner, `Range#sum` is now O(1), update of ForkJoin library, Fixes in immutable TreeSet/TreeMap, Improvements to PartialFunctions).

---

[96]http://docs.scala-lang.org/overviews/core/value-classes.html
[97]http://docs.scala-lang.org/sips/pending/implicit-classes.html
[98]http://docs.scala-lang.org/overviews/core/string-interpolation.html
[99]http://docs.scala-lang.org/overviews/core/futures.html
[100]http://docs.scala-lang.org/sips/pending/type-dynamic.html
[101]http://docs.scala-lang.org/sips/pending/modularizing-language-features.html
[102]http://docs.scala-lang.org/overviews/parallel-collections/overview.html

Design Patterns in Scala

Design patterns are a great way to make your code functional, readable, and extensible. There are some patterns that are easier and require less code in Scala compared to Java.

Strategy Pattern

The Strategy pattern involves changing a small bit of functionality within a larger context. Scala is excellent for this approach since it treats functions as first-class citizens of the language.

Imagine you have three different methods for finding totals:

```scala
def totalPricesLessThan10(prices: List[Int]): Int = {
    var total = 0
    for (price <- prices)
            if (price < 10) total += price
    total
}
def totalPricesMoreThan10(prices: List[Int]): Int = {
    var total = 0
    for (price <- prices)
            if (price > 10) total += price
    total
}
def totalPrices(prices : List[Int]) : Int = {
    var total = 0
    for (price <- prices)
            total += price
    total
}
```

The only part of the above three functions that changes is the decision of which price to include. This could be achieved by a function that takes in a price (Int) and returns a Boolean. The solution in Scala might look like this:

```
1  def totalPrices(prices: List[Int], selector: Int => Boolean): Int = {
2          var total = 0
3          for (price <- prices)
4                  if (selector(price)) total += price
5          total
6  }
```

The function type `Int => Boolean` represents a function that takes one Int parameter and returns a Boolean. Now you can call the above method three different ways to achieve the desired results:

```
1  totalPrices(prices, { _ < 10 })
2  totalPrices(prices, { _ > 10 })
3  totalPrices(prices, { true })
```

Iterators

Scala has multiple ways to iterate through collections. There is the imperative approach that is most familar to Java programmers:

```
1  for (i <- 0 until args.length) {
2    println( args(i) )
3  }
```

Although you can iterate this way in Scala, it is generally not recommended. Instead you should use the more functional approach:

```
1  args.foreach { arg =>
2    println(arg)
3  }
4  //or just
5  args.foreach(arg => println(arg))
6  // or even
7  args.foreach{println}
```

You can also use:

- `map` – Converts values.
- `flatMap` – Converts values and then concatenates the results together.
- `filter` – Limits the returned values based on some boolean expression.
- `find` – Returns the first value matching the given predicate.

- `forAll` – True only if all elements match the given predicate.
- `exists` – True if at least one element matches the given predicate.
- `foldLeft` – Reduces the values to one value using the given closure, starting at the last element and going left.
- `foldRight` – Same as foldLeft but starting from the first value and going up.

For example, you can use `map` to perform an operation on a list of values:

```
val list = List(1, 2, 3)
list.map(_ * 2) // List(2, 4, 6)
```

DSL's

Scala has a very flexible syntax, which makes it great for writing DSL's (Domain Specific Languages):

- Parenthesis and dots (.) are optional in some situations.
- Ability to add methods to classes using Traits and implicits.
- The ability to override any operators (plus, minus, etc.)

For example, you could create a DSL for calculating speeds with specific units, such as Meters per second.

```
val time = 20 seconds
val dist = 155 meters
val speed = dist / time
println(speed.value) // 7.75
```

This is a simple example, but it demonstrates many of the features possible in a Scala DSL.

You can override operators very simply in Scala. By overriding operators, you can constrain users of your DSL to reduce errors. For example, `time / dist` would cause a compilation error in this DSL.

Here's how you would define this DSL:

```
1    class Second(val value: Float) {}
2    class MeterPerSecond(val value: Float) {}
3    class Meter(val value: Float) {
4      def /(sec: Second) = {
5        new MeterPerSecond(value / sec.value)
6      }
7    }
8    class EnhancedFloat(value: Float) {
9      def seconds = {
10       new Second(value)
11     }
12     def meters = {
13       new Meter(value)
14     }
15   }
16
17   implicit def enhanceFloat(f: Float) = new EnhancedFloat(f)
```

Notice how the divide / operator is defined just like any other method.

We used `implicit def` to enhance the Float type. We will discuss implicits in the next section.

Metaprogramming in Scala

Scala has the `implicit` keyword, which allows the compiler to do implicit conversions for you. For example, the following Scala code will automatically call `makeRobo` on a Person if `crushCars` is called on a Person:

```
1    class Person{
2      def eatDonuts = println("yum")
3    }
4
5    class RoboCop(val person:Person){
6      def this() = this(new Person)
7      def crushCars = println("smash")
8    }
9
10   object Person{
11     implicit def makeRobo(person:Person):RoboCop = new RoboCop(person)
12     implicit def makeNormal(robo:RoboCop):Person = robo.person
13   }
```

You have to create the Person object in addition to the Person class (this is called a companion object in Scala). Scala requires that you get those implicit functions (makeRobo, makeNormal) in scope and this is just one way to do that. Now you can do the following:

```
1    val person = new Person
2    person.eatDonuts
3    person.crushCars
```

The Scala compiler is smart enough to realize that since Person does not have the crushCars method, it looks for an implicit converting function that would make this code compile. Then it finds and inserts the makeRobo(person) function.

Since this can cause code to look somewhat "magical" implicit functions should be used sparingly.

The Scala Ecosystem

There are many different frameworks built on top of Scala that make up the Scala ecosystem. Here are some of them (in alphabetical order):

Web Frameworks

BlueEyes[103]
> A lightweight Web 3.0 framework for Scala, featuring a purely asynchronous architecture, extremely high-performance, massive scalability, high usability, and a functional, composable design.

Lift[104]
> A secure, scalable, and modular web framework for Scala.

Play framework[105]
> Play is based on a lightweight, stateless, web-friendly architecture built on Akka.

Scalantra[106]
> Tiny Scala Web framework, inspired by Sinatra.

ORM Frameworks

Activate[107]
> A plugable object persistence, supporting both ORM and NoSQL, plus STM.

MapperDao[108]
> ORM library that encourages clean domain model, type safe and with query DSL that resembles select statements.

SORM[109]
> A pure case-classes oriented ORM framework for Scala.

Squeryl[110]
> A Scala ORM and DSL for talking with Databases with minimum verbosity and maximum type safety.

---

[103]https://github.com/jdegoes/blueeyes
[104]http://liftweb.net/
[105]http://www.playframework.com/
[106]https://github.com/scalatra/scalatra#readme
[107]https://github.com/fwbrasil/activate

Build frameworks

Maven + maven-scala-plugin[111]

A Scala plugin for Maven.

SBT[112]

A build tool for Scala (used by Play and other projects).

SBuild[113]

A Scala-based build system for Java, Scala and almost any other build job with Eclipse Integration and Ant Task integration.

Testing frameworks/Code Analysis

ScalaCheck[114]

A powerful tool for automatic unit testing.

ScalaMock[115]

Mocking of objects and functions (formely Borachio).

ScalaTest[116]

Open-source test framework for the Java Platform designed to increase your productivity by letting you write fewer lines of test code that more clearly reveal your intent.

Specs2[117]

A BDD library for writing executable software specifications (superseding the original specs library).

Concurrency

Akka[118]

Actors, typed actors, remote actors, and transactors.

---

[108] https://code.google.com/p/mapperdao/

[109] http://sorm-framework.org/

[110] http://squeryl.org/index.html

[111] http://www.scala-tools.org/mvnsites-snapshots/maven-scala-plugin/

[112] http://www.scala-sbt.org/

[113] http://sbuild.tototec.de/sbuild/projects/sbuild/wiki

[114] https://code.google.com/p/scalacheck/

[115] http://scalamock.org/

[116] http://www.scalatest.org/

[117] http://etorreborre.github.com/specs2/

GridGain[119]

High Performance Cloud Computing, Community Edition.

Kestrel[120]

Tiny queue system based on starling, in scala.

Menthor[121]

Menthor is a framework and abstraction for distributing/parallelizing iterative algorithms common to fields like machine learning and convex optimization.

Honorable Mentions

Kojo[122]

The Kojo Learning Environment.

Rex[123]

Regular expressions DSL.

ScalaNLP[124]

Useful routines for natural language processing (NLP) and machine learning.

---

[118]http://akka.io/

[119]http://www.gridgain.com/

[120]https://github.com/robey/kestrel

[121]http://lcavwww.epfl.ch/~hmiller/menthor/

[122]https://code.google.com/p/kojo/

[123]https://github.com/KenMcDonald/rex

[124]http://www.scalanlp.org/

Part III: The Web

JVM Clouds

Cloud is a much hyped term, but what it boils down to is the natural progression of services supporting web-development. As the internet economy grows, so do services supporting that economy. The size of the economy running on JVM-supported web-development is huge and ever-expanding.

Here are just *some* of the best JVM PaaS (Platform as a Service) vendors (in alphabetical order):

- Cloudbees
- CloudFoundry
- Heroku
- Jelastic

Cloudbees

Cloudbees[125] runs a host of different PaaS services, including a continuous integration (build) service using the Jenkins build manager. They also host SVN or git code repositories and have free accounts (for <= 2GB and <= 3 users).

CloudFoundry

Cloud Foundry[126] was originally founded by Chris Richardson, author of "POJOs in Action". It was then bought by Spring, which was bought by VMware. Cloud Foundry supports a lot of languages and frameworks, including Scala, Play, Spring, Grails, node.js, and Rails.

As well as being a hosted service offered by VMware, Cloud Foundry is also an Open Source project. Other companies also offer PaaS services using the Cloud Foundry platform. Examples include:

- Uhuru Software[127] is one company that has created an AppCloud using Cloud Foundry. Uhuru's PaaS provides support for multiple frameworks (.NET, Rails, and Spring) and languages (Java, Ruby, PHP, and C#).
- AppFog[128] hosts their PaaS on Amazon Web Services, OpenStack and Windows Azure.
- ActiveState[129] is a company that has created a commercial distribution of the Cloud Foundry software for enterprises to host their own private PaaS.

---

[125]http://www.cloudbees.com/
[126]http://cloudfoundry.com/
[127]http://www.uhurusoftware.com/
[128]http://appfog.com/
[129]http://www.activestate.com/stackato

Heroku

Heroku[130] is owned by Salesforce.com[131]. Heroku was one of the first cloud platforms and has been in development since June 2007. When it began it supported only Ruby, but has since added support for Java, Scala, Groovy, Node.js, Clojure and Python. Heroku supports multiple tiered accounts, including a free account.

Heroku relies on *git* for pushing changes to your server. For example, to create an app in heroku using the CLI do the following:

```
1  $ heroku create
2  $ git push heroku master
```

Your app will be up and running and heroku will tell you the URL where you will find it.

Jelastic

Jelastic[132] is a winner of the 2012 Duke's Choice award and a favorite of Java-creator James Gosling. It runs your Tomcat, database (Postgres, MySQL, or MongoDB) and only charges you for what you "use" (on average and only in certain increments). However, your free trail only lasts about 14 days, so be prepared to pay after that.

Commonalities

Every JVM PaaS promises to make deployment easier. They take care of your hardware, JVM, web-container (like Tomcat), and your persistence solution (MySQL, Postgres, MongoDB, Redis, etc.). Each has at least a CLI (Command Line Interface) and web console for easy configuration and monitoring. Some, like Cloudbees, even have an Eclipse plugin.

Payment is based on an incremental system. This gives you much more flexibility than running your own hardware stack. All of these clouds also have free accounts with minimal resources (unless otherwise noted).

---

[130]http://www.heroku.com/

[131]http://news.heroku.com/news_releases/salesforcecom-signs-definitive-agreement-to-acquire-heroku

[132]http://jelastic.com/

Grails

What is Grails?

Grails is a web-framework for Groovy that follows the example of *Ruby on Rails* to be an opinionated web framework with a command-line tool that gets things done really fast. Grails uses convention over configuration to reduce configuration overhead.

Grails lives firmly in the Java ecosystem and is built on top of technologies like Spring and Hibernate. Grails also includes an Object-Relational-Mapping (ORM) framework called *GORM* and has a large collection of plugins.

Quick Overview of Grails

After installing Grails[133], you can create an app by running the following on the command-line:

```
1  $ grails create-app
```

Then, you can run commands like `create-domain-class` and `generate-all` to create you application as you go. Run `grails help` to see the full list of commands available.

Grails applications have a very specific project structure. The following is a simple break-down of *most of* that structure:

- **grails-app** - The Grails-specific folder.
    - conf - Configuration, such as the Data-source and Bootstrap.
    - controllers - Controllers with methods for index/create/edit/delete or anything else.
    - domain - Domain model; classes representing your persistent data.
    - i18n - Message bundles.
    - jobs - Any scheduled jobs you might have go here.
    - services - Back-end services where your back-end or "business" logic goes.
    - taglib - You can very easily define your own tags for use in your GSP files.
    - views - Views of MVC; typically these are GSP files (HTML based).
- **src** - Any utilities or common code that doesn't fit anywhere else.
    - java - Java code.
    - groovy - Groovy code.

---

[133]This overview is based on Grails 2.1.4, but the basics should remain the same for all versions of Grails.

- **web-app**
  - css - CSS style-sheets.
  - images - Images used by your web-application.
  - js - Your javascript files.
  - WEB-INF - Spring's `applicationContext.xml` goes here.

To create a new domain (model) class, run the following:

```
1  $ grails create-domain-class
```

It's a good idea to include a package for your domain-classes (like `example.Post`).

A domain class in Grails also defines its mapping to the database. For example, here's a domain class representing a blog post (assuming User and Comment were already created):

```
1   class Post {
2       String text
3       int rating
4       Date created = new Date()
5       User createdBy
6
7       static hasMany = [comments: Comment]
8
9       static constraints = {
10          text(size:10..5000)
11      }
12  }
```

The static `hasMany` field is a map which represents one-to-many relationships in your database. Grails uses Hibernate in the background to create tables for all of your domain classes and relationships. Every table gets an `id` field for the primary key by default.

To have Grails automatically create your controller and views, run:

```
1  $ grails generate-all
```

Grails will ask if you want to overwrite existing files if they exist. So be careful when using this command.

When you want to test your app, you simply run:

```
1  $ grails run-app
```

When you're ready to deploy to an application container (eg. Tomcat), you can create a "war" file by typing:

```
1  $ grails war
```

Plugins

The Grails ecosystem now includes over one-thousand plugins. To list all of the plugins, simply execute:

```
1  $ grails list-plugins
```

When you've picked out a plugin you want to use, execute the following (with the plugin name and version):

```
1  $ grails install-plugin [NAME] [VERSION]
```

This will add the plugin to your project. If you decide to uninstall it, simply use the uninstall-plugin command.

What's New in Grails 2.0?

There have been a lot of great changes in Grails 2.0:

- Grails docs are better.
- Better error page - shows code that caused the problem.
- Database console at <app>/db
- Grails 2.2 supports Groovy 2.
- Runtime reloading for typed services, domain classes, src/groovy and src/java
- Run any command with -reloading to dynamically reload it.
- Binary plugins - jars
- Better scaffolding - HTML 5 compliant (mobile/tablet ready).
- PageRenderer and LinkGenerator API for services.
- Servlet 3.0 async API supported - events plugin - platform core
- Resources plugin integrated into core.
- Plugins for gzip, cache, bundling (install-plugin cached-resources, zipped-resources)
- New tags: img, external, javascript

GORM API (grails-data-mapping)

- Supports: MongoDB[134], riak[135], Cassandra[136], neo4j[137], redis[138], Amazon SimpleDB
- New, compile-time checked query DSL
  - aggregate functions supported: avg, sum, ...
  - subqueries, .size(), etc.
- Multiple scoped data sources.
- database-migration plugin - for updating production Databases.

Testing

- Better unit testing: mixin approach.
- `@TestFor(X)` `@Mock(Y)` - Domain -> In-memory GORM = `ConcurrentHashMap`
- Tests for Tag libraries, command objects, URL-Mappings, XML & JSON, etc.

Cache plugin

- You can add the `@Cacheable` annotation on Service or Controller methods.
- cache tags – `cache:block`, `cache:render`
- cache-ehcache, -redis, -gemfire
- Cache configuration DSL.

Grails wrapper

```
1  $ grails wrapper
```

The above produces `grailsw` and `grailsw.bat` (for *nix and Windows respectively).

The Grails wrapper is helpful when multiple people are working on a project. The wrapper scripts will actually download and install grails when run. Then you can send these scripts to anyone or keep them in your repository.

---

[134] http://www.mongodb.org/

[135] http://wiki.basho.com/

[136] http://cassandra.apache.org/

[137] http://neo4j.org/

[138] http://redis.io/

Cloud

Grails is supported by the following cloud providers:

- CloudBees[139]
- CloudFoundry[140]
- Amazon[141]
- Heroku[142]

Only an Overview

This has only been a brief overview of Grails. Many books have been written about Grails and how to use it. For more information on using Grails, please visit grails.org[143].

Groovy Mailgun in Heroku

Learning a bunch of theory is nice, but sometimes it's helpful to see a real-life example. For this purpose, let's implement a Grails service for sending emails from an application running in the cloud.

Let's use the Mailgun[144] with Groovy on Heroku. Although you might think sending emails is easy, it's not if you don't want your email to end up in the SPAM folder. Mailgun provides a SaaS (Software as a service) for sending and receiving emails with free accounts available. To make things interesting we're going to use Mailgun's REST api.

First of all, you need to import a bunch of classes and declare your service and the `sendEmail` method:

---

[139]http://www.cloudbees.com/

[140]http://www.cloudfoundry.com/

[141]http://aws.amazon.com/ec2/

[142]http://www.heroku.com/

[143]http://grails.org/

[144]http://www.mailgun.com/

```
1   import org.apache.http.*
2   import org.apache.http.entity.*
3   import org.apache.http.client.*
4   import org.apache.http.client.methods.*
5   import org.apache.http.impl.client.*
6   import org.apache.http.params.*
7   import org.codehaus.groovy.grails.plugins.codecs.URLCodec
8
9   /** Uses MailGun to send emails. */
10  class EmailService {
11
12          static API_KEY = System.env.MAILGUN_API_KEY
13
14      def sendEmail(to, subject, text) {
```

Second, you need to add the encodeAsURL method to Object's metaClass. You'll use this later for encoding the parameters.

```
1   final codec = URLCodec.newInstance()
2   Object.metaClass."encodeAsURL" = { -> codec.encode(delegate) }
```

Then define your API url and parameters:

```
1   def url = 'https://api.mailgun.net/v2/your-app.mailgun.org/messages'
2   def params = [from: "you@email.com", to: to, subject: subject, text: text]
```

Next, create the *DefaultHttpClient* and *HttpPost* with credentials and headers:

```
1   def httpclient = new DefaultHttpClient()
2   def post = new HttpPost(url);
3   def creds = new UsernamePasswordCredentials('api', API_KEY)
4   post.addHeader(BasicScheme.authenticate(creds, "US-ASCII", false));
5   post.addHeader("Content-Type", "application/x-www-form-urlencoded");
```

Lastly, encode the parameters, join them, and put them in the post.

```
1  def list = []
2  params.each {k,v -> list << "${k}=${v.encodeAsURL()}" }
3  post.entity = new StringEntity(list.join('&'))
4  def response = httpclient.execute(post);
5  response
```

That's it, you're done! Now you can send emails easily (Mailgun's free service comes with up to 300 emails/day).

Using other REST services in the cloud (such as Twilio) with Groovy is very similar.

The full gist[145] of EmailService is available on github.

---

[145]https://gist.github.com/3996601

Play Framework 2

What is Play?

Play is a web-framework for building scalable, asynchronous web-applications using the Akka concurrency model. Play 2 can work with either Scala or Java, although we're going to assume you're using Scala for now.

Quick Overview of Play

After installing Play, you can create a new app by running the following on the command-line:

```
1   $ play new
```

Play applications have a very specific project structure as follows:

- **app** - Source code of your application.
  - controllers - Controllers that defines Actions.
  - views - Scala-based view templates that produce HTML (by default).
- **conf** - Configuration files and data, such as routes.
- **project** - Project build scripts.
- **public** - Publicly accessible static files.
  - images - Images used by your web-application.
  - javascripts - Javascript files.
  - stylesheets - CSS files.

Play includes all of the pieces necessary to build a web-application, including an HTTP-server, so you don't need to run your application inside a container. You can start your application at anytime by typing:

```
1   $ play run
```

The Play welcome page should appear at http://localhost:9000/.

Controllers, Views, Forms

Much like in Grails, controllers define the actions that can take place and which views are used. Scala has functions that correspond to HTTP codes such as OK:

- Success: return ok(...)
- Error: return badRequest(...)

Views are based on templates. The default template language is Scala-based. For example, here's an html page with a title that shows the environment's user and the date:

```
1   @(title: String)
2   @import play.api.Play.current
3   <!DOCTYPE html>
4   <html>
5   <head>
6     <title>@title</title>
7   </head>
8   <body>
9   user: @current.configuration.getString("environment.user"),
10  date: @(new java.util.Date().format("yyyy-MM-dd HH:mm"))
11  </body>
12  </html>
```

The first line of the file is much like a parameter list for the view template.

ORM

Play does not include an ORM solution like Grails does. You will need to include your own, such as Squeryl[146] to interface with a database.

Play 1.x

Play was radical when it came out. It used a dynamic development cycle (automatic compile & reload), was containerless, and used actor-based asynchronous threading. It started out without Scala and even supported Python at one point. However, Play 2.0 is a different animal.

---

[146]http://squeryl.org/

Play 2.0

Play 2.0 was released Feb 2012. Play 2.0 added a lot of features including the **sbt** build tool, the (Akka[147]) library for concurrency, and concentrated more on the Scala language. It has the following features:

- Development console for RAD.
- Type checked all the way (route files, templates, Javascript).
- Support for asynchronous programming techniques (webSockets, streaming, Comet and Eventsource, akka).
- Support for front end tech: LESS, Clojure, require.js, coffeescript
- Functional test runner
- Web helpers (async HTTP client, form validation, Oauth, ORM, etc.)

Play is built on Netty, akka, Java, Scala, and HTML5 web sockets. Play is extensible; you can make your own templating/routing implementation. Java and Scala can coexist. Play has a huge community and plugins (~60 plugins) and the ability to test with a mock browser and in-memory database.

Typesafe Activator

Typesafe created the Activator to help you more easily learn the Play framework. It is currently at version 1.0 and works with Play 2.2. After you download it, you simply start the ui with the `activator ui` command.

The Activator runs in your web-browser. It will give you the option to start a project from one of many project templates. It has a built-in editor and tutorial on the right-hand side. It's an easy way to learn the many different facets of the Play framework.

 ## Only an Overview

This has only been a brief overview of the Play 2 framework. At the time of writing, there is a book covering this topic in more detail, "Play for Scala"[148]. See playframework.org[149] for more information.

---

[147]http://akka.io/

[148]http://www.manning.com/hilton/

[149]http://www.playframework.org/

RESTful web-services

REST stands for REpresentational State Transfer[150]. It was designed in a PhD dissertation and has gained some popularity as the new web-service standard. Many developers have praised it as a much better standard than SOAP (which we will not attempt to describe).

At the most basic level in REST, each CRUD operation is mapped to an HTTP method:

- Create: POST
- Read: GET
- Update: PUT
- Delete: DELETE

The transport mechanism is assumed to be HTTP, but the message contents can be of any type, usually XML or JSON.

The JSR community has designed the JAX-RS API for building RESTful Java web-services, while Groovy and Scala both have some built-in support for XML and JSON and various way of building web-services.

REST in Groovy

Groovy includes some support for XML, such as the XMLSlurper.

Grails includes converters for simply converting objects to XML or JSON or vice versa.

```
1  import grails.converters.JSON
2  import grails.converters.XML
3
4  class BookController {
5          def getBooks = {
6                  render Book.list() as JSON
7          }
8          def getBooksXML = {
9                  render Book.list() as XML
10         }
11 }
```

For REST services that service multiple formats, you can use the built-in withFormat in Grails. So the above would become:

---

[150]http://www.ics.uci.edu/~fielding/pubs/dissertation/top.htm

```
1  def getBooks = {
2       withFormat {
3              json { render list as JSON }
4              xml { render list as XML }
5       }
6  }
```

For *using* web-services in Grails, there's a rest plugin[151] available.

REST in Scala

There are several options for writing REST web services in Scala. Scala itself provides first-level support for XML literals so you can write your own XML conversions[152].

Lift has built-in support for REST[153].

Play provides built-in parsers for JSON and XML, and a simple DSL for creating JSON[154]. For example:

```
1  import play.api.libs.json.Json
2
3  object Application extends Controller {
4
5      def books = {
6          Json.obj(
7            "books" -> Json.arr(
8              Json.obj(
9                "name" -> "PostgreSQL Up and Running",
10               "authors" -> "Regina Obe & Leo Hsu"
11             ),
12             Json.obj(
13               "name" -> "REST API Design Rulebook",
14               "authors" -> "Mark MassÃ©"
15             )
16           )
17         )
18     }
19
20  }
```

---

[151]http://www.grails.org/plugin/rest
[152]http://joeygibson.com/2009/09/24/im-liking-scalas-xml-literals/
[153]http://simply.liftweb.net/index-Chapter-11.html
[154]http://www.playframework.com/documentation/2.1.1/ScalaJson

JAX-RS 1.0

JAX-RS 1.0 (the Java API for RESTful Web Services) was defined in JSR-311[155].

It has many implementations, including the following:

- CXF[156] - a merger between XFire and Celtix (an Open Source ESB, sponsored by IONA and originally hosted at ObjectWeb).
- Jersey[157] - the JAX-RS Reference Implementation from Oracle.
- RESTEasy[158] - JBoss's JAX-RS project.

JAX-RS defines a set of request method designators for the common HTTP methods: `@GET`, `@POST`, `@PUT`, `@DELETE`, `@HEAD`.

When a resource class is instantiated, the values of fields and bean properties annotated with one the following annotations are set according to the semantics of the annotation:

- `@MatrixParam` - Extracts the value of a URI matrix parameter.
- `@QueryParam` - Extracts the value of a URI query parameter.
- `@PathParam` - Extracts the value of a URI template parameter.
- `@CookieParam` - Extracts the value of a cookie.
- `@HeaderParam` - Extracts the value of a header.
- `@Context` - Injects an instance of a supported resource.

Gotcha's

- If a subclass or implementation method has any JAX-RS annotations then all of the annotations on the superclass or interface method are ignored.
- If you're using Spring AOP on your web-service classes, this interferes with the ability of your JAX-RS library to get your annotations. Either all of your methods should be added to the interface or CGLIB proxies have to be explicitly enabled (consult Spring AOP documentation for more details).

JAX-RS 2.0

JAX-RS 2.0 adds a lot of new features to the REST API and comes with Java EE 7. It adds a client API, asynchronous processing for client and server, filters and interceptors, and some HATEOS features.

---

[155]http://jcp.org/aboutJava/communityprocess/final/jsr311/index.html

[156]http://cxf.apache.org/

[157]https://wikis.oracle.com/display/Jersey/Main

[158]http://www.jboss.org/resteasy/

Client API

JAX-RS 2.0 adds a client API to the standard.

You can use the `ClientFactory` to produce a `Client` and then a `WebTarget`. For example:

```
1   // Default instance of client
2   Client client = ClientFactory.newClient();
3   // Create WebTarget instance base
4   WebTarget base = client.target("http://example.org/");
5   // Create new WebTarget instance hello and configure it
6   WebTarget hello = base.path("hello").path("{whom}");
7   hello.register(MyProvider.class);
```

Then, to execute on the Web Target do the following:

```
1   Response res = hello.pathParam("whom", "world").request("...").get();
```

This would result in a GET request on the URL `http://example.org/hello/world`.

Asynchronous Processing

Asynchronous REST API calls were added as a first-class feature to JAX-RS. This allows the REST client to issue multiple requests in parallel and the server to handle such requests.

- Server API support
    - Offload I/O container threads
    - Suspendable client connection
    - Leverage Servlet 3.x async support (if available)
- Client API Support: `request().async().get( callback )`

Filters & Interceptors

On the server-side you have two different types of filters:

- `ContainerRequestFilter` runs before your JAX-RS resource method is invoked.
- `ContainerResponseFilter` runs after your resource method.

On the client side you also have two types of filters: `ClientRequestFilter` and `ClientResponseFilter`. ClientRequestFilters run before your HTTP request is sent to the server. ClientResponseFilters run after a response is received, but before the response body is unmarshalled.

Filters are useful for cross-cutting features, such as:

- Logging
- Security
- Compression

While filters modify request or response headers, interceptors deal with message bodies. Interceptors are executed in the same call stack as their corresponding reader or writer. There are two interceptor interfaces:

- ReaderInterceptor
- WriterInterceptor

Interceptors can be used to add digital signatures or "gzip" message bodies for example.

Sometimes you want a filter or interceptor to only run for a specific resource method. You can do this with a @NameBinding annotation. Annotate a custom annotation with @NameBinding and then apply that custom annotation to your filter and resource method.

```java
@NameBinding
public @interface MyFilterBinding {}

@MyFilterBinding
public class MyFilter implements ContainerRequestFilter {
        /* code... */
}
```

Then, in your RESTful Service:

```java
@Path
public class RestfulService {

        @GET
        @MyFilterBinding
        public String get() { /* code... */ }
```

HATEOS

JAX-RS 2.0 adheres more closely with REST principles and includes features of HATEOS[159] (Hypermedia as the Engine of Application State).

---

[159]https://en.wikipedia.org/wiki/HATEOAS

For more on the topic of HATEOS you might consider reading the book "REST API Design Rulebook" by Mark Masse or "RESTful Web APIs" by Richardson, Amundsen, and Ruby.

It includes the following:

- Id's & Links
- (RFC-5988[160] Web Linking) - Link types: Structural, Transitional
- Use @Produces to define what is returned:

```
1  @GET
2  @Produces("text/plain", "text/html")
3  public Widget getWidget();
```

 For more information, see JSR-339[161].

---

[160]http://tools.ietf.org/html/rfc5988
[161]http://jcp.org/en/jsr/detail?id=339

Final Thoughts

The State of the JVM

The JVM provides a robust platform for software development. In addition to Java, we've covered two of the most prominent languages targeted at the JVM: Groovy and Scala.

Java 7 included `invokedynamic` for enhancing the performance of dynamic languages on the JVM, like Groovy. Meanwhile Groovy added optional type-checking.

Java 8 will bring the most anticipated feature to Java: lambda expressions. However, most of the advanced features of non-Java languages, such as operator-overloading and mixins, will probably never come to the Java language, for better or worse. Many of these features can already be achieved by using other JVM languages like Groovy and Scala.

Project Jigsaw[162], which was deferred to Java 9, will make the JVM modular.

The Future

A wise man once said, "Prediction is very difficult, especially about the future."[163] At the same time, everyone depends on some prediction to survive and thrive. As programmers, we depend on varying levels of certainty in the future of technology, be it Java, the JVM, or the continued improvement of hardware.

In this spirit, we look forward to some big trends on the horizon such as big data, RESTful web-services, the "web of things", wearable computing, machine learning, and parallel programming. As we tackle these problems of the future, it's likely that our tools (including languages) will evolve to meet these new challenges.

Hopefully this book served as a tiny nudge in the right direction. It was only meant as a brief introduction to many different tools and languages that hopefully spurred you to learn more about them.

Contact the Author

If you have any comments or suggestions, please go to adamldavis.com[164] and click "Ask me anything."

---

[162]http://openjdk.java.net/projects/jigsaw/

[163]https://en.wikiquote.org/wiki/Niels_Bohr

[164]http://adamldavis.com/

Appendix: Groovy for Java Devs[165]

Feature	Java	Groovy
Public Class	public class	class
Loops	for(Type it : c){...}	c.each {...}
Lists	List list = asList(1,2,3);	def list = [1,2,3]
Maps	Map m = ...; m.put(x,y);	def m = [x: y]
Function Def.	void method(Type t) {}	def method(t) {}
Mutable Value	Type t	def t
Immutable Value	final Type t	final t
Null safety	(x == null ? null : x.y)	x?.y
Null replacement	(x == null ? "y" : x)	x ?: "y"
Sort	Collections.sort(list)	list.sort()
Wildcard import	import java.util.*;	import java.util.*
Var-args	(String... args)	(String... args)
Type parameters	Class<T>	Class<T>
Concurrency	Fork/Join	GPars

No Java Analogue

Feature	Groovy
Default closure arg.	it
Default value	def method(t = "yes")
Add method to object	t.metaClass.method = {}
Auto-delegate	@Delegate
Extension methods	Categories
Rename import	import java.util.Vector as Vect

Tricks

Feature	Groovy
Range	def range = [a..z]
Slice	def slice = list[0..3]
<< Operator	list << addMeToList
Cast operation	def dog = [name: "Fido", speak:{println "woof"}] as Dog
GString	def gString = "Dog's name is ${dog.name}"

---

[165]Version 1.3 of this cheat-sheet.

Appendix: Scala for Java Devs[166]

Feature	Java	Scala
Public Class	public class	class
Loops	for(Type it : c){...}	c.foreach {...}
Lists	List list = asList(1,2,3);	val list = List(1,2,3)
Maps	Map m = ...; m.put(x,y);	val m = Map(x -> y)
Function Def.	void method(Type t) {}	def method(t: Type) = {}
Mutable Value	Type t	var t: Type
Immutable Value	final Type t	val t: Type
Null safety	(x == null ? null : x.y)	for (a <- Option(x)) yield a.y
Null replacement	(x == null ? "y" : x)	Option(x) getOrElse "y"
Sort	Collections.sort(list)	list.sort(_ < _)
Wildcard import	import java.util.*;	import scala.collection._
Var-args	(String... args)	(args: String*)
Type parameters	Class<T>	Class[T]
Concurrency	Fork/Join	Akka

No Java Analogue

Feature	Scala
Default closure arg.	_ (underscore is positionally matched)
Default value	def method(t:String = "yes")
Add method to object	use Trait
Auto-delegate	use Trait
Extension methods	implicit class
Rename import	import scala.collection.{Vector => Vect}

Null, Nil, etc.

Type	Description
Null	A Trait with one instance, null, similar to Java's null.
Nil	Represents an empty List of zero length.
Nothing	A Trait that is a subtype of everything. There are no instances of it.
None	None signifies no result. Option has two subclasses: Some and None.
Unit	Type to use on a method that does not return a value.

---

[166]Version 1.3 of this cheat-sheet.